D0913877

SENDING

AN ATHLETE CONFRONTING CANCER

BY JENNIFER ERIN PINKUS

Dedicated to
Jen's amazing friends

Sandor (1948-2018)

Cary and Barbara Wolinsky
for their kindness

Aaron and Maggie
who will carry Aunt Jenny's memory
in their hearts

TABLE OF CONTENTS

SENDING

Should I quit no I should send
If I fall I will just have to get up again.
Look for feet and keep moving up
Will that bolt hold my weight
I heard Ibuprofen will make me feel great
Look for feet and keep moving up
Will that third Camelot hold
Percocet will work I am told
Look for feet and keep moving up
Will that .75 stay in the crack
Will the Rituximab fix my back

Look for feet and keep moving up
Will that nut catch me if I fall
Will the Adriamycin make my lymph nodes small
Look for feet and keep moving up
You either send or you die
With that outcome you might as well try
So if you fall
Place your feet and keep moving up
Because you have no choice
But to
Send

MY STORY

On April 7th, I was diagnosed with cancer. On the 17th, I had a biopsy and a port put in. On the 20th, I was told I have something called follicular lymphoma. It is a type of blood cancer that can be managed, but I will have it for the rest of my life. It is unclear what my treatment will be and when it will start.

I apologize for not explaining what was going on earlier, but as you can imagine, I have been scared, in disbelief and overwhelmed with decisions. It all seems surreal and like a bad movie, not something that is really happening to me. I have had chronic back pain and some sharp cramps in my side, but I never ever expected this.

Meanwhile, I read all your kind words and so appreciate your many good wishes. Know that if I do not respond to calls or emails, it is only because I am not feeling well or just cannot talk about my situation at that moment.

Please do continue to keep me in your thoughts, as I believe that will help me recover. I do not know what I will need, but will let you know as I begin this process.

Thanks again for being wonderful. I am so grateful to be surrounded by such amazing people!

CU BIOPSY

May 6, 2015

I JUST CAME BACK from a bone marrow biopsy at CU. I am feeling OK. I was scared, but it was not as horrible as I expected. The day was long. I couldn't eat, drink or take Percocet. I didn't realize how much I needed the Percocet or, at least, Ibuprofen. It took a while to do the blood work, but the biopsy itself was quick and fairly painless. We'll see if I feel that way tomorrow.

I have a few infections so I have to take antibiotics before I start treatment. I will meet with a lymphoma specialist next Thursday at CU and get a second opinion on the best approach for me. There are two options, an antibody called Rituximab or chemotherapy. They each have their advantages and disadvantages. Both will have major side effects and involve several treatments and two years of follow up infusions.

It is hard to envision this as I feel bad, but not that bad. It is hard to believe that getting sick will make me better. It is much easier to put it off! Can't I just eat kale and drink Kombucha? I did get permission to bike and climb while waiting for the stitches from the biopsy to heal. I am hoping that I can be active in between treatments. Most likely they will be on Mondays at Shaw and I will start on the 18th. I will keep you posted.

Thanks again for all your support.

BEING DIAGNOSED

May 10, 2015

JUST THE OTHER DAY I was climbing at Homestake, biking in Eagle and teaching ski school. I think you have made a mistake. Cancer is something that you read about in books or see in bad movies, not something that happens to me. I feel just fine except for a bad back.

When I went to the Dr., I just wanted pain pills or a referral for PT. I am young, healthy, and in shape. None of this makes sense. And now you have left me hanging. I have to sit at the cancer center alone while you put dye into my body and then send me into a machine to think for another hour.

Three days of lab tests and I have a week to play while waiting to hear whether I will live or die. That makes free time really fun! On top of it, I've got to decide what to do about jobs and insurance and then hear everyone's death and survival stories and wonder which one will be me.

Now, I have stitches from my biopsy and a port on my left side. I didn't mind waking up to the biopsy bandages. I cried when I saw the port. My stoic boyfriend dropped me off, picked me up, and held me when I called my parents and cried.

What did I do to deserve this? Was it the gummy bears, microwaving my coffee all the time, talking on the phone or am I being punished for being a bad person? If I had only eaten less sugar or stayed away from electrical items. I wish I had eaten more broccoli and had been more giving.

I think of all the times I could have been there for friends, but I went climbing, or biking, or worked instead. I am being taught a lesson not to complain and be so critical, but to appreciate what I have. Couldn't it have happened in an easier way? I wish I could take back every moment I have been frustrated or unkind to anyone then maybe I wouldn't be sick.

Email messages pour in and friends text and I remind myself to live for the moment. You are here now and your only choice is to fight. "God only gives you as much as you can handle," I am told over and over again. I am not religious, but I pray that I can handle the poison that is going to be put in my body every week and I pray that I can be mentally strong enough to get myself through this.

I read all my responses on Facebook and think of what to write. I think of my parents and my sister and my boyfriend and what they must be thinking. I crawl into bed and curl up in Sandor's arms and cry.

THE DAY AFTER BEING DIAGNOSED

May 11, 2015

ANOTHER DAY FEELING like the world is surreal. Feeling like this can't really be happening to me. Scared, sad, tired. Scared to eat. Scared to talk in case I jinx my situation. Scared to respond. Too much information from everyone. My head hurts. I don't know who to go to and feel like I can't breathe. When will the doctor call to give me the results of the biopsy?

How did I miss the call? The most important call of my life and I didn't hear it ring. Now I have to call back. The hardest call I will ever make. I am scared. I want to know, but I don't want to know if it means I am going to die. Do I go out tonight with friends? Do I hang out at home since I feel awful physically and mentally? What if this is my last night to ever go out? How will I tell my parents? How did this happen?

"Dr. D., this is Jen." "We have your results, Jen. The good news is your cancer is manageable. The bad news is it will never go away. I gave you the analogy that Hodgkin Lymphoma is a 1 out of 10 to pick out of a hat. You got an 8 out of 10 (with Non-Hodgkins). You're going to live, but you're going to be scared every time something bothers you for the rest of your life."

Do I cry or is this good news? It is called follicular lymphoma. Old people get it. Not young people. Why me? It is the most common non-Hodgkins lymphoma. The treatment might not be as aggressive as we thought, but you might have to have the treatment more than once. It will be chemo or it will be antibodies administered as an infusion.

Sandor says I am a trooper. I have won two of the battles so far. Don't question the results. Wait until you meet with the oncologist to find out more. You are going to live. I am the pessimist, still having trouble digesting the information. Not understanding why it is in my body.

All these texts. All these people who care, who call me. I am so lucky, but I need a night to think about the diagnoses and figure out how to share the new. I want to understand better what this means before I respond. At the same time, I am afraid to read about follicular lymphoma because there are some things that I would rather not know.

My heart is less scared, but I am still so frightened. My world was flipped over, twisted and turned in less than an hour and now forever.

SCARY THAT I AM GETTING USED to going to Vail Valley Medical Center. Everyone there knows me and stops to ask if I have been climbing, biking and if I need anything. It is nice. Still rather not be there, but am so appreciative that they take the time to care.

I have come for a second ultrasound on my aching butt. Once again with a no solution outcome. Something else is wrong as the pain is keeping me up at night more than the cancer. My left side looks way bigger than my right and it feels like I am sitting on a baseball. Driving is the worst and sleeping is just not happening.

The result was that I should look into getting a biopsy on my butt in Denver or take more Percocet. Hope I will get more answers tomorrow as I would like the pain to get better at some point. It isn't like I don't have enough problems to deal with.

I meet with Dr. M. tomorrow at CU for a second opinion. Hopefully she will clarify which is the best approach to dealing with the cancer; Rituximab alone or chemo plus Rituximab. I would like to rehash the positives and negatives of both and then ask what she would choose. I know ultimately it is up to me. I hate that about medicine. I wish it was black and white! I do not need more choices!

Meanwhile I am sitting on my right butt trying to figure out what to do about my summer job and insurance.

What a nightmare it is to make decisions when you don't know what your next few months hold. Wish there was a little fairy that could just make all these decisions for me!

THANK GOODNESS FOR FRIENDS

May 13, 2015

THIS IS HARD IN EVERY ASPECT. It is hard to play, hard to love and hard to sleep.

I had a good weekend. It was my birthday and some friends threw me a party. It was so nice of them! Everyone has rallied and I feel so lucky. Also, it got my mind off of everything for a while, especially after a glass of red wine.

Rode with friends Saturday morning. I RODE. Yeahhhh!! I have to get adjusted to being last and feeling like I am going to die. Sooo not me! But I made it! I was in pain, but it felt great to be on my bike. The girls were wonderful always reminding me that it is about having fun. I need to just appreciate that I can ride, live in the mountains, be with my friends and not worry about keeping up.

After the ride, I had a big beer at the Brewery. My friends got normal glasses and I got the Birthday massive mug. I drank maybe 5 sips. Don't think the bartender was too impressed. Oh Well! The day felt like some semblance of normalcy to my otherwise not so normal existence right at this moment. That night, Sandor and I had a nice dinner at Terra, our go-to restaurant. Saw the Terra crew. Got a birthday dessert with my name written in a pretty cursive.

On Sunday, I got to ski some backcountry. Once again my friends were patient while I huffed and puffed and tried to drink water. My face was on fire from the antibiotics and 14,000ft felt like 20,000ft, but I made it! I am lucky to have patient friends. Patience is something I need to learn.

Inside I am conflicted about whether to play or rest as my first treatment is scheduled for Monday. Sandor is wonderful. He always has my best interest in mind. I realize he is going through what I am going through with me. I thank him, but don't want to burden him or owe him. I don't want him to have to take care of me, but I don't know if I will be able to take care of myself. It scares me.

ThRoBBinNg!

May 13, 2015

MY BUTT IS THROBBING! ThRoBBiNg! It could be my fault as I went climbing yesterday. Didn't feel too bad during the day, but tonight OUCH!! Gotta' take a nap...one sentence...will continue...

OK...next sentence. (Twenty minutes later.) Took another Percocet. Can type now. This is probably the most Percocet I have taken in one night since I got diagnosed. Maybe climbing is not such a good idea especially at Boulder Canyon where the hikes are steep and Tyroleans require lots of strength. But I love it!! It is my therapy!

I have become a total rookie as I am at everyone's mercy. I know I should just appreciate having great friends that are strong climbers and will put up all the routes for me, but it makes me feel helpless. Even when I am not sick, I am not a leader and the only way I will get better is by climbing, which is just not an option right now.

Despite my frustration at my abilities, thank goodness for my friends who constantly distracted me from thinking, kept me going, and praised me as I tried my best at everything. I am so lucky to have positive people who continue to support me throughout my struggle.

I work my ass off all winter and I save and save only to spend all my money on broken necks and knees in May. And now this. While everyone is out climbing in the desert, riding in Fruita, or off to Rifle, I am in and out of the hospital and trying to substitute teach in between taking Percocet and not sleeping.

Sandor is great. He reminds me this is not permanent and that these things I get upset about are really not what is pertinent right now. I am sick. Healing is most important. Sports will be there. Right now I have to focus on getting better not trying to keep up. I am lucky to have what I have. He is so wise. Why can't I be that wise? I know these things, but easier said than done.

Thank goodness I go into the hospital tomorrow. I need to fix my butt. It is still ThRoBBiNg!! Attempt to sleep number 9!

UNIVERSITY OF COLORADO AGAIN AND ANOTHER BIOPSY

May 14, 2015

APPARENTLY, there is a tumor in my butt. Hence the reason I feel like I am sitting on a grapefruit and can't sleep at night. It is pinching my sciatic nerve. The doctors saw something in the PET scan, but my butt didn't hurt then so we let it go. Now I wish we had caught it earlier because it really throbs.

I was starting to be OK with what was going on and now I am scared again. What if this tumor is not the same kind of cancer? What if it is faster growing? Now they will have to change the treatment plan again. Please God make it be the same cancer and do not make me have a tougher chemo. And please let me keep my hair!

Once again, I hope that this doctor at CU, Dr. K., will clarify what is going on in my butt and in my stomach. Hopefully, she will give me the negatives and positives of both treatments. Pray that it is nothing worse. I don't think that I can handle more bad news.

Then I start chemo treatment on Monday. I guess this is all really happening.

WTF

May 14, 2015

IT WENT FROM STAGE I to stage IV. How can this be?!?!!

IT WENT FROM STAGE I to stage IV. How can this be?!?!!

Apparently, my indolent cells have now combined with aggressive cells that are forming tumors and cysts around my body. The Rituximab that we were going to use to treat the indolent cells meant that the side-effects were supposed to be tolerable and I would still be able to keep my hair.

I will now have to have something called R-CHOP, which involves more chemicals, more side effects, and will cause my hair to fall out. I was very upset about the initial diagnosis, but was learning to deal with it. This is way worse.

Damn butt! Just doesn't seem fair. I remind myself that it could always be worse, but somehow that saying I usually use doesn't apply to this situation.

I have an EKG at 11 tomorrow and then start R-CHOP chemo on Monday. I then go back to Denver for another biopsy on Wednesday. I know they say try to keep life normal and not get overtaken by cancer, but please tell me how.

COMMENTS

Hi Jen
We are sending lots of love and big hugs your way. You are strong and beautiful inside and out. Love,
> —Nancy, Alan, David and Leah, May 14, 2015

Jen. You are in my thoughts. Your strong body is going to help you get through this! I am sorry you are in so much pain in addition to everything else that's going on. I know decisions haven't ever been your forte, but glad you have Sandor as your rock! Hugs
> —Rachel, May 14, 2015

Jen— you are strong and beautiful!!! Keep up being positive. I am here with you the whole time. Lots of love to one badass chica!!!
> —Mia, May 14, 2015

PRE-CHEMO

May 16, 2015

TODAY WAS A LONG DAY. I started with an EKG at the Vail Valley Hospital that showed my heart to be normal. Thank goodness something is normal. I watched the ultra sound tech carefully, trying to read her expression. She probably thought I was crazy.

Katie, the nurse, was great as I was more than overwhelmed and in tears as she explained the many side effects from chemo. I get to look forward to nausea, mouth sores, chance of infection, loss of hair, hot flashes, skin rashes, and possible shock and blood poisoning from the Rituxen. Lovely!

Then I got to meet with the social worker to try and figure out my job situation and once again came to no conclusion. It is hard to decide whether to work when you don't know what you can and can't do.

And the catch is you might get disability pay, but you don't know until after you have paid COBRA and not worked for 6 months. Thanks, Colorado for your help!

Luckily, the sun came out and I got a special window of opportunity, just for me, to take a quick and therapeutic lap on Berry Creek. Thank you weatherman! It was much needed. Exercise makes everything better. I could then refocus to repeat to my family what they should expect.

Might need to ride all day Sunday so I won't freak out the night before chemo. I just have to keep reminding myself to live for the moment and don't think about the "what ifs." Try to be positive. You can do it. I don't want to lose my hair.

WIGS

May 16, 2015

Jen
You are a strong and amazing person!!
I am sending positive thoughts your
way!!!! I agree with your friend, cut it
short to get used to it and then buzz it.
We could have a "buzzing" party with my
two guys who usually get a summer buzz
around this time.
    —Danielle, May 17, 2015

Hey GF. I would go with a rad new look.
Purple sounds fun. Why not? And I think
you will look gorgeous with no hair. So
don't fret that. And we can have cool hat
parties?
    —Mia, May 16, 2015

Curls!! Curls!! Curls!! You know my vote :-)
    —Sister, May 16, 2015

SO I BROKE DOWN and looked at wigs last night. As upsetting as it is, I actually had a few good laughs with Sandor. It took me a while to figure out that the prescription for a cranial prosthesis was for a wig. After watching Oprah on Letterman, we giggled that I could get Oprah hair or even go purple or pink as that seemed to be a fad with the wig companies that supply cancer patients.

In the end, I went to bed and woke up at 2 a.m. having nightmares about the poison being put into my body on Monday. Thank goodness for friends again as my skype rang just in time to cheer me from being stuck in my bad dream. I am lucky to a have a few friends who have survived cancer and are my main cheerleaders and advice givers.

One happens to be in Thailand where it is perfect timing for me to skype when I can't sleep because it is mid-afternoon there. Her smiley face and only baldish head re-assured me that it will be OK. Amy is exercising, eating, traveling, and her red hair is slowly coming back in, softer and more beautiful. She is healthy and alive. She tells me there are wigs at The Cancer Center and to cut my hair short this week to get used to it. Then buzz it before it starts to fall out and make me depressed and itchy.

I believe this is hard for everyone, but especially someone like me who is pretty set in my ways and who has had nothing but a trim pretty much all of my life. As my friends know, I keep my skis, bike, car until they are barely functioning. I have lived in the same house or condo and pretty much had the same jobs most of my Vail life. Needless to say, change scares me. Especially this change.

I emailed some friends and have some numbers for hairdressers to buzz my head. I am hoping they can do it after hours so I can cry, hide and then wait a few days to go out. Please remember if I get fat, bald or look weird because I lost my eyelashes and eyebrows or have bags under my eyes, I am still me. Treat me like me please!

I think I will do blond (more Jennifer Anniston hair) as I am not sure purple suits me!

STILL PLAYIN'

May 17, 2015

I MUST BE MEANT TO WRITE at 2 a.m. because going to sleep is not happening. My butt is throbbing and my mind is swirling quickly and in every color. Maybe, Sandor was right about playing too hard. I hurt! However, it is worth it to get to climb, be focused and in my element for just a few hours.

Thank you, girls! You are the best! You helped me get my Homestake fix for one last day of climbing before chemo. I got to lead and TR a bunch of routes and just feel good about myself for a while. I didn't think about my situation, smiled, and laughed!! Thank you, thank you, thank you. I think we all needed it today.

We have to appreciate what we have and live in the moment because things can change so quickly. I am sad and terrified. However, I feel lucky I have a home, support, the mountains, and a chance to fight this disease.

Bad things happen all the time, sometimes terrible things to good people who do not deserve them. Celebrate the good memories. Hold those in your heart. Meanwhile, do what makes you feel alive. Make more memories. Be strong, vibrant, and happy. Laugh, love and go climb rocks.

THE DAY BEFORE MY FIRST TREATMENT

May 18, 2015

MOM IS HERE! I have been trying to stay busy, not think. It is hard when it is rainy out. I keep worrying about what I have not gotten done as if this is my last day to live. Then I have to remind myself to think positive. I am going to survive this and will probably have a lot of time to get stuff done: medical stuff, job stuff, BILLS (YUK)!

I gymmed it, climbed, ran (kind of) and then grocery shopped with Mom. I walked Minion with Andrea and got some fresh air. Glad to have pretty places to walk and good company to walk with. Don't think! Thank you those who have texted and called and reminded me I am tough and going to win this battle. It is what I need to hear. I am going to post my schedule on the calendar so you can see when I am at Shaw and when I am at home (probably Sandor's)

I need things to be dumbed down, kept silly and as light as possible considering the weight of the situation. Visit me pre or post treatment and make me laugh or just listen please! If I don't call or you come by and I am sick, I apologize ahead of time. Either I am too tired or have too many calls. It is not because I don't love you. It might be because Sandor shut my phone off and said rest and talk to me!

I've gone through my checklist: filled out and signed all the forms, got the numbing cream for my port, got the Allopurinol to get rid of chemical bi-products, and got the Prednisone for pain, swelling and energy. That's five pills with breakfast. I chose a comfy outfit for the day and a few junk magazines. Got my book of questions and the HUGE, black book that I am supposed to carry with me. I have my purple water bottle so I can drink at least 3 liters a day.

I am going to dinner to stay busy. No thinking! No thinking! Stay calm! Wish for the best. Thinking of Son of Middle Creek and winding past the creek and across the bridge. Think of cruising through the flowers at the top of Two Elk or reaching the anchors on Wolfman's Shuffle. Think about my aunt's beach house that I will visit when this is all over and a powder day out on OS with no one around, but me.

It will all be OK. No thinking! Get these bad cells out of your body!!

MADE IT UNTIL 4AM!

May 18, 2015

MADE IT UNTIL 4AM this morning, but am now downstairs in the extra room silently freaking out. Note to self, do not look up information on the computer about treatment. It most always will make things worse. I want to know, but I don't. The stages are more complicated than I thought, but I am stage IV bad. Lalalala...skip this article!

Everyone says work, stay busy. You're tough. You can do it! Thanks, I need the cheers and encouragement, but what if I can't be tough this time? Sometimes being tough makes things worse. For example, anyone else would have known that they had an infection the size of a grapefruit in their leg, but not me! I just thought I must have fallen and gotten a bruise. A cut right now could be dangerous!

All the people on the internet who have endured RCHOP say it is the worst of all the treatments and work will be impossible. They have mouth sores, infections, numb toes and fingers, nausea, stomach sickness, hot flashes, and write about going mentally crazy. They say the risk of infection is too high and your body is too weak to work. How do you know? What do I do? Maybe I get a job from home. Writing.

I want to stay busy but I will have no immune system if I get an infection. I don't want to make a promise I can't keep. I don't want to get sick though. Do I hide and stay in my room and avoid people? I feel like I am headed to be electrocuted this morning and I am innocent! I took a Percocet. Please, Percocet, knock me out!

I don't want to do this. I start taking Prednisone this a.m. Please be patient with me if I am sad, irritable, fat, angry, spacey (I know I already am some of these things). I hate drugs. Why would anyone take them just for fun?

POST CHEMO

May 18, 2015

I AM FEELING OK. It wasn't as bad as I thought. I just feel tired and a little hung over. I am trying to be optimistic. I am also trying to keep things in perspective as I know my cancer will get better with treatment, but my reaction to the treatments will get worse as the toxins build up in my body. I'd rather be prepared for the worst and be pleasantly surprised if the worst doesn't happen than not be prepared and shocked by my reaction to the meds.

Dr. U. was patient and answered my questions at the beginning of the visit. We went back to the treatment room and Leesa, my nurse, was wonderful. She hugged me, introduced me to the other nurses and explained to me exactly what would happen. First, Lees would flush my system with saline, then I would get the Acoxi to prevent nausea. Next, the three chemo drugs, one which would make me pee red and then she'd flush my system one more time before I go home.

I came equipped. I had my BIG black book, purple medical binder, novel, ipad, music, Mom and Sandor. Over the course of four hours, I did not pull out any of those items. We talked a bit, looked at photos, met all the other nurses and I repeated my name and birthday each time a new drug was administered. Focusing would have been quite hard as it is already a challenge for me and I had to pee like every ten minutes!

I was prepared all day to be sick, dizzy and in shock. Instead I was just scared! I am tired and feel like I had too many margaritas. That is why they say alcoholics tolerate chemo well.

When I got home, I took a walk around the block and a hot bath and am feeling better. Again, just scared. I suppose that being scared is just going to have to be my new norm for a while. I will have to find a way to push my fear to the back of my mind and live on.

Meanwhile The Voice is on to take my mind off of everything. I am collecting any cute hats and looking for a flexible job that I can do from home if anyone has any suggestions. Tutoring is always good; I can take kids climbing at the gym, love to write and edit, or do anything creative or school curriculum related. I just can't be in a crowded place with germs.

Addendum:I take back the not so bad. I am hot, nauseous, and bloated, but not throwing up! I am scared to eat or drink anything in case of mouth sores. I am staring at 100 different medicines that I could add to my liquid doses of chemo poison: Percocet, Compazine (nausea), Allopurinol (kidney stuff), Senna (counteract constipation from the Percocet). Do I add to the mixture or eat bread and drink ginger ale for another hour? Bread and ginger ale, I think.

CONQUERING THE RITUXIMAB/ THINKING BACK ON MY FIRST CHEMO

May 19, 2015

I MADE IT!! Oh, my goodness what a scary day. I had it in my head that I was going to go into shock, throw up everywhere, and have the chills all day. When the chaplain came in, I thought he was here to give me my last rites. I was not planning to make it through the day, but I am alive.

This is not to say that it was fun. I spent most of the day staring at the bag and holding my chest thinking at some point my heart was going to leap out of my body. I drank water like it was going out of style, took my rack with all my infusions (that I call Bob Roll because it bobs and rolls) with me to the bathroom every ten minutes and tried to eat oatmeal biscuits at lunch time.

I did have great visitors who tried to keep me distracted, which was great! I met the nutritionist. Sandor left for that part. I think he is nutritioned out, as I have been a bit obsessive about what I need to do to save myself. I guess kale and Kampuchea can't replace chemo. There are lots of common sense healthy suggestions. Unfortunately, there are few studies of their effect on lymphoma.

Katie, the nurse, came in just to check in on me and Kathy, my chemo nurse, waved to me through the window every few minutes. Mom, Sandor and Kathleen visited me in the afternoon. I fought taking the Benadryl so that I could stay awake as I wanted to be alive for every minute before my heart leapt out of my body.

Once again I did not touch my black bag of stuff. I'd much rather have good people to distract me. I slept for a bunch of hours when I got home and actually ate a decent meal. Things do taste a little metallic. Certain things disgust me like meat and chocolate! Chocolate! Oh, No! I have been craving weird things like sourdough bread and suckers. I have a little bit of a headache and am on my fourth liter of water and taking Tylenol.

One more hospital day in Denver tomorrow. Hopefully, my last biopsy. Then I get a few weeks of normalcy. It is amazing how I went from working, playing, and stressing over what to do for the weekend to going from medical center to medical center, shopping for wigs, and trying to figure out medical benefits. I am hoping I can work a little and play a little before my next treatment and take a break from thinking about being sick!

3am update: Bllghhhh, everything tastes like metal except Sourdough bread! Got a few hours of sleep but life is back on my mind; to work or not work, another surgery today, health insurance. It will be a treat to sleep through the night someday.

SO SICK/ON THE WAY TO DENVER FOR A SECOND BIOPSY

May 20, 2015

SO, SICK.

OK, I can write now. Thank goodness for Tums, Compazine, Percocet, ginger ale and loaves of Artisan bread. What a great cocktail. So much for being into traditional medicine and eating healthy.

I think that might have been the longest car ride of my life! Even longer than flying home from Philly and driving to Vail with the norovirus. The ride down was fine. I was a little queasy from my breakfast of colorful pills, but not too bad. The drive back was another story.

I get spoiled in Vail where the nurses and doctors are always checking in on you. In Denver, they stuck me in a room by myself, thirsty and alone, and didn't come back forever. They got the IV all messed up, taped it on like crazy, and then each nurse I saw after the first grabbed it, twisted it, and tugged at it again.

They hardly sedated me before the biopsy, which was fine, but really painful afterwards. The sound of them cutting a sample of the lymph nodes made me ill. I think next time I will allow them to fully sedate me. My morning dose of Prednisone makes me so parched that all I could think of was juice. Should have been careful for what I asked for. After downing two cups of cranberry juice, I was told that I could not get up to pee until the sedation wore off in a half hour or so.

I begged the nurse to let me take my mom to the bathroom with me. Losing the battle, I had to succumb to peeing in a bed-pan. The nurse seemed annoyed that I could not hold it. I wanted to suggest to her to try Prednisone for breakfast. Needless to say, I left feeling OK and relieved.

We stopped at the wig store, which made me want to cry. I did find one that seemed like it would work. I had trouble making it fun and laughing over my options as losing my hair was definitely not in my lifetime plans. Unfortunately, the drive home after leaving the wig shop did not go so smoothly.

I am not sure why, but my body lost it. I was hot, cold, nauseous and then everything else. The Idaho Springs stretch was the worst. I took a Compazine and tried to stare out the window. Then we entered a huge cloud from Georgetown to Frisco and I just prayed that I could keep everything in my stomach going down Vail Pass.

I could feel my incision; my head was pounding and my body ached like I had been run over by a car. Thank goodness for Sandor and my mom staying calm, driving fast, and then dropping me off and running to the store to get me Tylenol and more bread. A loaf of bread, Tums, a Tylenol and 12 hours of sleep later and I am feeling better.

I am still having hot flashes, but can type this journal. No more biopsies for a while please!!

SO MUCH BETTER!

May 21, 2015

COMMENTS

Great to hear you feel better You must look wonderful with your new hair and hat. Kids send you lots of hugs and best wishes!!!! Us too!!! Hope you have a good weekend! Saludos
   —Edith, May 22, 2015

Hi jenny. I am so happy that you have stretches of time when you are feeling better. I love you sweet cousin!
   —Cousin Betsy, May 22, 2015

So glad to hear you are doing better! Makes me happy! Let's see a photo of your haircut! Xoxo
   —Rachel, May 22, 2015

WOW! I FEEL LIKE A NEW PERSON TONIGHT. I don't know if it is because I felt so awful the last few days or because I truly feel good. Either way I'll take it! I probably slept over 15 hours last night and this morning and woke up still queasy and a million degrees.

After a short walk, a cinnamon bun, and my morning drugs, I actually began to feel pretty normal. Mom and I ran errands and I bought a cute hat at Walmart. We went to Shaw so they could take my labs and I tried on a few more wigs. I am still a bit in denial over the wigs. I did however get my hair chopped at 3:30.

I got my friend Kerri at Hair by Kerri to cut it so I would look like Meg Ryan. She made me laugh, cry, and look beautiful for a few weeks. I came home to a package from my sister and all my favorite friends bearing organic gummy bears, bath soaps, good stories, and kind words. How wonderful. I am so lucky!

Thank you, for all the wonderful calls, messages, and texts. It really means so much to me! On the Mondays and Tuesdays after chemo, it is so great to know you care, even if I can't respond. Thank you again and again. I had a wonderful dinner with Sandor and actually ate something besides bread. I am ready to curl up under my blankets and sleep with my new Meg Ryan haircut. At least, I like to think I look like her, even if it is just for a few days.

Until 2:30: Nights suck. I can taste and smell the chemicals. They gross me out. I feel like I eat, sweat, and pee them. I probably do. At least, during the day I am moving so they are flushing through my system. At night, it feels like the meds are sloshing around in me and dripping onto my sheets and pouring out of my head. Blughhhh!! All I can think to do is get up, eat bread (specifically Italian bread), drink ginger ale until I pee it out, and take a Percocet so I can try to fall asleep. Mint oil under my nose is working too, it makes me forget about the other tastes and smells. YUUUKKKKK!!!

NOTIFICATION NUTS/MY PURPOSE IN WRITING

May 23, 2015

I WANT TO THANK THOSE OF YOU who are reading my writing, as I know it is journally. I am not sure what my purpose in writing is quite yet. I think it is to help me feel better, to keep those interested updated, and to allow me to share with you what is happening so I don't get depressed repeating it on the phone. I was also hoping it might help me track my story, give me a goal that I can control (since I feel out of control of the cancer) and possibly help others who might be going through this today or in the future.

A quick re-cap of yesterday. It was a pretty good day. I worry on good days whether to enjoy them or whether they are a tease. I guess the answer is enjoy them when they happen and don't be disappointed if the next day is not as easy. My game plan is to set realistic expectations and be prepared for anything. I don't want to be overly positive and then get let down.

The cancer, "knock on wood," is dying down a bit. The electric shocks are occurring with less strength and less frequency. The tumor in my butt also seems significantly smaller! I even have to remind myself it is still there, as I have been weaning myself off Percocet, but still need a half a pill or so every once in a while or a sudden wave will hit me hard. That is way better than 2 pills and two Ibuprofen every 4 hours and a fat ass!

I didn't taste the chemo drugs as strongly yesterday, but they are there. I feel a need to always be eating something. I know that is not unusual, but this is extreme. Even if I am stuffed, I need to have the taste of food in my mouth and not the taste that is there when my mouth is empty. I have a smorgasbord of flavored suckers and am still pounding down the everything baguettes and ginger ale. Weird, but seems to work.

I did make it to Target yesterday with Mom, after laughing over old videos of me and my sister from when we were kids. Even then my hair was longer than it is now :(I felt good most of the day, but a bit tired. That was OK as I was shopping for patio chairs, so I just napped in each one that I tried. It was a typical Walmart trip and I came back with a skirt, socks, Werthers candy and a loaf of bread. No chairs, Oh well! Maybe chairs will go on sale this weekend.

When we got home, I made my backyard loop two times and even ran a little bit when it started to hail-rain-snow as it does here. Never just one event. It was exciting. I am having a little trouble breathing. I don't know if it is from the cancer or just being out of shape from doing nothing all week. Either way I am psyched to attempt to ride my bike this weekend if the weather holds up.

We went to half -price sushi at Nozawa (yum) with great company. I know I have said it to exhaustion, but I have the greatest friends and family ever.

Curt and Marly made me smile, told me my hair looked great, even though it makes me want to cry, and reminded me they are here if I need them. Pretty cool!!! Thank you!!

Sandor, of course, remains my rock and diehard hero, even though he would kill me if he ever read this blog. He has put his life on hold and put me above and beyond everything else. He has taken me to all my appointments, sat by my side while I cried, and held me while I had the chills and felt nauseous.

My family has called, sent me packages, and cried with me, always letting me know they love me and are here for me. My fabulous, fabulous friends and neighbors keep waving and smiling and emailing and making me laugh. Please don't stop as this is going to be a long battle and you are helping more than you know. I thank each one of you from the bottom of my heart.

GUESS WHAT I DID TODAY?

May 23, 2015

COMMENTS

Rock on Jen. How cool to have had such a successful bike ride. What a great attitude to approach your good days—milking then for every good moment you can. We are with you good days and bad!
 —Sam, May 24, 2015

I am glad you had such a good day. Your writing is marvelous my strong, beautiful daughter.
 —Mom, May 23, 2015

I RODE MY BIKE. I went all the way up Battle Mountain and felt good. I timed it perfectly. I had two hours of sun before black clouds circled in from the west. I got home just before the hail began and the sky crashed down with thunder. Lucky!!

I can't believe how OK I felt considering what my body has been through the last few months. I had no plans to make it to the top. Maybe I rode well because my legs are fresh, I probably weigh ten pounds less or because I have less hair on my head. I don't know but I was excited! I guess we can withstand more than we think.

Mornings are still rough. I think all the bad stuff that is in my body settles when I am still at night and makes me ill when I wake up. But once I get going, I do pretty well. I even made it to Home Depot after riding and ran errands with Sandor. One errand landed us next to the new pot store Rocky Road.

They were offering pot Pepsi for $4.20 at 4:20 as a Memorial Day Special. I was not interested in the Pepsi, having enough drugs in me. However, I am a lame Coloradan and have still not been in a pot shop. So, I ventured in. Holy Cow!!! It is like walking into a fancy bar with marble floors, fancy counters, cigars in glassed- in cases, and people dressed like they were going to the opera. I felt like I was in a Robert De Niro movie.

I did start to feel a little bit of electricity around 5pm, so I took a half of a Percocet and did some yoga before taking my first bath in forever. Every time I am given permission to take a bath, which is great for relieving my pain, I have to have a biopsy and am not allowed to submerge myself in water. What a treat it was. I just soaked and soaked until the water was cool. Then I added more hot!

If I can have a few decent days like this, I will be OK. I feel rejuvenated. A little tired, but I don't want to lie flat. However, I am feeling Lancesque and ready to ride or climb again tomorrow, weather permitting.

Hopefully, I will also be able to work a little bit again next week. Maybe there can be some normalcy in between the craziness!

ANOTHER GOOD DAY

May 25, 2015

FEELING BETTER. I don't want the good days to end!

I haven't quite returned to pre-chemo form, but I am starting to feel more functional. My nights still seem to go from 11-2 and then 5-9. It takes me a while to get all the stuff in my belly out and get moving in the morning, but coffee drinkers would say that happens to them every day. I still crave weird foods like Cheez-Its, sourdough bread, cranberry juice, and I taste metal all day. But once I get going, I do OK.

Unfortunately, today I had to go to a funeral for an amazing person (kid, 21) who should not have died so young. It was a sad, but beautiful memorial. Someone wrote a post about our community that I thought summed up Vail beautifully. "Many of us have rivers in our blood, snow in our dreams, and summits in our souls; that is why we live here. We work hard and play hard, we take care of each other, and when we lose one, it is deeply felt by all." Logan's death put my chance to live in perspective. I wish I could give this opportunity to him.

I was a bit exhausted after the memorial, more from emotion and lack of sleep than sickness. I took a short nap and then got motivated to go to the gym. I feel a time constraint to play and be happy before I am knocked down again. Physically, I feel better than I have all week. Mentally, however, I am having trouble focusing.

I had forgotten about being sick all morning. Unfortunately, going out usually means bumping into friends and being reminded. For some reason, I went into panic mode at the Vail Activity Center and fell down the stairs. My lace got stuck in the steel and I hit, face first, five steps down from where I started. A man helped me up as I burst into tears over such a non-significant fall. Stressing over my cuts and bruised leg, I cried, "I can't get hurt right now. I just can't! Just what my body needs as my blood counts drop!" The poor guy. I'm sure he wrote me off as crazy!

I have become a paranoid freak. I hid over by the climbing wall for the rest of the afternoon. I had it to myself. I planned this purposefully, avoiding crowds since my immune system is at its lowest these next few days. Also, I did not want to be questioned. I cruised around and even got vertical on the wall. I felt good.

I watched the sun peep through the clouds outside the window and decided I needed some Vitamin D. I stopped at the store for an emergency bread. Then drove to my favorite trailhead still wanting to fit everything in while I feel good. I decided to try to run; well, I guess it was more like a skip-jog. I chased the light up the North trail knowing it would dissipate and be blanketed with the mist coming from the South within an hour. Where are our 100 days of sun?

Being alone allows way too much time for me to contemplate my situation. I did well on the way up because it hurt too much to think, especially after tumbling down the stairs. On the way back, I allowed my mind to return to the dreaded, "Should I work?" "Which health insurance is best?" I can't believe I have to do chemo again on the 8th. I hit a rock and spun down the hill. Dang!!!

Laying low tonight. I have decided venturing out might be dangerous in my state, so we made homemade stromboli and I'm cooking a last batch of chocolate chip cookies as I type. Domesticated activities are surely much safer than running or walking downstairs.

Rereading this journal, I'd say I had somewhat of a normal day or at least the most normal I have had in a while. Besides my brain being preoccupied, a few trips, and some minor stomach issues, I'd say I was rather productive. To someone normal it might have been a bad day, but not for me. I only took two pills, Allopurinol and Percocet. I climbed, ran, ate, baked, and cried a little too.

I don't want today to end because I am scared about what the next day will bring.

FEELING GUILTY

May 26, 2015

AGAIN, A TWO-DRUG DAY; Allopurinol and Percocet, what a deal!

I am feeling a little bit guilty for all this attention when I felt so healthy today. I didn't even wake up feeling sick. I had big Memorial Day ski plans and was prepared to ski no matter what! The cool thing was, there really was no "matter what."

I was a little nervous to go an hour drive away and a 2-3 hour hike after this last week, but was feeling pretty good. Molly came to pick me up around ten and we ventured off to pick up Sarah and head up to the base of Climax Mine, which probably sits at around 10,500ft. Skins—check, boots—check, poles—check. I can't believe it is snowing. The peaks are fully covered and it is almost June!

Oh well, guess we might as well ski. The snow was icy and wet down low. We did a beacon check and Sarah and Ben dug a pit at around 11,500 to observe the snow pack. It got increasingly more consolidated as we gained elevation. Towards 12,000ft we hit a false summit or I guess a summit depending on your destination. We could see Climax Mine, Mt. Democrat, and all the other peaks surrounding us. It was like a painting with white-capped mountains peeking through the dark clouds swirling to the west of us.

We twisted our way between rocks, kick turning up the ridgeline, towards the pitch we had decided to ski.

Recent tracks meander in the same direction and were windblown but easy to follow. The rock went from a beautiful orange and green granite to a shimmery mica schist. We de-skinned at around 13,000ft and took a second to look at the view.

I felt good the whole way up! I did eat a loaf of bread and take a half a Percocet up top, but probably would have eaten the loaf of bread regardless. All I could think of was FUCK this cancer thing. I just skinned 3000 vertical feet and am about to make fresh turns down a long couloir dropping in at 13,000ft. We had started climbing around 11:30 and it was now 2:00 and I felt great!

Wanting to chill, we decided we should wait and do that at the bottom due to the impending wall of blackness headed towards us. Ben dropped first, Sarah second, then Molly, then me. I had luscious, smooth turns brushing along the side of the already tracked snow to where I could make my own path. We stopped periodically throughout to check in and decide the safest line to ski.

The snow went from cold, skiddy S turns to a pretty smooth stretch of easy turning to a little denser hard to push through snow. Then towards the base came the heavy, thick mashed potato mush that wants to grab you. We laughed as we all struggled through the flattest easiest section, the wet snow jerking us to a standstill, as we tried to get enough momentum to make it to the summer road.

What a day! Three hours up and less than a half an hour down. Guess that is how it goes! I have appreciated each adventure this week more than I ever have in the past. Each one a feat in its own way.

Pain gives you a new appreciation for life. After dropping everyone off, Molly and I stopped at The Northside for a drink and started talking to the donut guy. "I'm throwing them all away at the end of the day so help yourselves."

We left with bags filled with Fruity Pebbles donuts, chocolate sprinkled donuts, glazed lemon filled donuts, and cinnamon buns. Just what the doctor ordered! Ended the evening with yoga and steam at the VAC. I felt like I was on vacation. I was feeling guilty beginning to write this, as it was a pretty cancer free day.

I was thinking throughout the hike that maybe the doctors would say they misdiagnosed me at my next visit.

POEM

May 27, 2015

AFTER BEING UP EVERY NIGHT for the last month, I just thought I would share a little poem. Sorry it is not pleasant. I have been scared all week anticipating the results of the last biopsy and after a half hour wait at Shaw, Dr. Alec arrived to tell me they did not get the results yet. Not that that is bad, it just means more anticipation. And I am tired. I wake up every night to metal and heat and nausea. I take back the guilt from my last entry as the feel- good days are warranted for the other non-feel good days.

I know this medicine is saving me and the cancer is the poison, but here is how I feel about the chemo.

POISONED

I just want to say SCREW the Vincristine
The red blood colored liquid that poisons your pee

The Rituximab with mouse hormones and the acronym RCHOP
That burns and makes everything smell and taste like chemicals
Chemicals that wouldfry the paint off a piece of metal
And leave it scorched like my body
An acronym that was never in my vocabulary
and that I want out

Goodbye to Prednisone
Five pills a day with Allopurinol, Calcium, and Senna
A breakfast cocktail that should entail coffee
A slice of bread and juice

COMMENTS

Jen
You amaze me with each entry. Your writing and your poetry are beautiful and you are so generous in sharing everything with us. I'm glad you find it helpful.

Glad also that you have the good days to help you through the rough ones. I'm amazed what you can do in one day when you're not at your peak—holy moly, you accomplish more in a day than I do in a year. Good for you for milking every minute.

Even if you were a beached whale we would love you. Much love and good thoughts to support you through the hard days. It's not forever even if it feels that way. XO
    —Sam, May 27, 2015

Not pleasant, perhaps, but on point and powerful. Praying for you, Jen! Enjoy the good days, and be strong through the bad ones. One day at a time...
    —Jill, May 27, 2015

ANOTHER EVENTFUL DAY

May 27, 2015

COMMENTS

Hi Amelia Bedelia,
Glad to hear that the Dead at least
helped to mellow out Sandor a little bit
and the packages made you smile. Lots
of love from LA,

  —Cousin Mark, May 28, 2015

I WAS THINKING THAT I should only write during treatments or if some other major health event occurs, but I feel like every day of my life seems to be eventful. This is not necessarily a good thing; for me it just is.

Somehow my life is like an Amelia Bedelia story. I guess everybody's life is a story, but maybe just a little less catastrophic than mine.

Again, down to two pills; Allopurinol, and Percocet. Things are actually beginning to taste a little bit less metallic and my bathroom time has become less all consuming. I was thinking if you added up all the time I sat on the toilet over the last month, and it was my job, I would probably have a pretty good paycheck. I am still parched most of the time, but nothing a little ginger ale, Gatorade, or a sucker can't fix.

I do have to say, as much as I do love not working, it would be nice to have some income and a forced rest since rest is not my forte! I do think God agrees with me as he/she keeps breaking my body. Why don't you just kick me while I am down? Really, I think someone is telling me to chill out and now it is official because my ankle is the size of a big pear.

There will be no biking or climbing tomorrow. I have been doing crazy things forever, way crazier than this week's activity. But for some reason, I am cursed this month. Sarah, Chris and I did five great climbs. We hiked 45 minutes up a rocky trail and I sprained my ankle spotting Chris as he started a climb. What the heck?? Come on now! First the stairs, then the trail run, and now this!

A sign, Sandor says. "Chill out! Stop trying to fit everything in and freaking out about work. You just have to be flexible and go with the flow for right now. Your job is to be safe, careful, and get better, not to be super human!" Dang it!!! Why does he always have to be so logical! This, from a man who can sit in a chair for hours listening to the Grateful Dead, speaking to me, someone who can't sit still for a minute.

Sandor is a great patient. Me, not so much! I do have to say, I am enjoying all the gifts and responses, mostly because it means so much to me that you guys all care. I am so lucky! I love hearing from everyone. I came home feeling pretty stressed to have disobeyed Sandor's "Chill out!" and now have another injury to add to the puzzle. Not only am I sick, but now I can't walk. Great! He is going to kill me!

In tears, I opened my door to a package full of Grateful Dead paraphernalia and pajamas. I automatically cheered up. Sweet! I can bribe Sandor with dancing bear shirts and maybe he won't even notice my ankle. Then I can curl up in my new cute PJ's and he won't be able to be mad at me. I think

I have the most amazing family and friends, and they're psychic! They know just what I need and when!

Unfortunately, it half worked. It gave Sandor the opportunity to share names, dates and Grateful Dead memories with me (that I have heard a million times). Usually, I am interested in the first two or three stories, but bored after five or six. This time I pushed him for more. But, the pain showed its face and I screamed for ice. I caved in admitting I was stupid, untrustworthy, and I was hoping he would find it in him to forgive me for being a punk.

He listened to the tears and apologies with little sympathy. I gave him his space to be angry with me. Maybe, tomorrow will be less eventful as I am banned from leaving the house.

POEM

May 27, 2015

RIDING

Tomorrow I will go for a ride
The trail will start steep and twist through the woods
It is a new trail so I will not know what to expect
Others have shared with me their experiences
But that is their ride not mine
It will get steeper and I will get tired
But I will continue to pedal
There might be rocks or mud puddles or bears
But I will ride carefully with determination
I will pass all of the obstacles
I might be scared and my body will continue to grow weary
But then I will see my destination
It might not be clear or might be a false summit
But it will give me hope and I will pedal towards it
And if it changes and I have to ride to the next peak
I will jump back on, exhausted, but with a second wind
And with support from nature
The power of the goodness that surrounds me
And will
I will continue
And if I have to
On and
On

LOSING MY HAIR

May 30, 2015

I SOMEHOW THOUGHT that I was going to defy chemo and be the one person who does not lose her hair. Crazy that two weeks after my first treatment, I am still in denial. It takes several treatments before your hair starts falling out so you can talk yourself into believing it won't happen. The first week I felt like a cancer patient. This week my sprained ankle hurts as much as the residual effects from the chemo. However, I know that next week when I lose my hair and have to prepare for chemo, I will feel sick again.

So, I broke down and tried on the wig that I have in a box again. They say day 14 is when hair usually starts falling out. That gives me two more days. I took tons of selfies so I have a few photos of me with hair, should I apply for a job or just need a normal picture of myself. I spent late last night and again just now on TLC Direct, Wigs for Cancer Patients. The doctors say my prescription for a "cranial prosthesis" works here. Go, doctors and your fancy complicated names!

I hated all the wigs at first. Then I decided to embrace the idea that I can be a red head, a blond, and even pink. I can have long hair, short hair, curly hair, or straight and I will never have to style it. Not that I do now! I found one curly haired Halo. I don't have to have a full head of hair and be ridiculously hot. I can just wear the piece with a cute brown hat.

Then I went to scarves because it hit me that I will probably get sunburnt if I have nothing on. Being totally au naturel could be harmful. The website has pretty paisley scarves, swim caps, and activity wraps, and even go to sleep twists. The site was like the chip aisle at the grocery store! You don't know where to start.

I picked out a few brown scarves to match my eyes. I figure, if I am not going to have eyebrows or eyelashes, I might as well bring out what is left. I read about how to cope with hair loss and all the blogs I could find on what to expect. I am still hoping I am going to defy history, but if not, I am prepared.

NOT READY YET!

May 31, 2015

COMMENTS

Your poems are beautiful!
—Ephraim, June 1, 2015

Jen, I'm so glad that we received your journal. Thank you for the updates, reflections and poems that convey so well the steps you must go through. My hair, too flew out the window, and perhaps was used for birds' nests. I hope so. When it grew back in it was wonderfully curly for a while, then straightened back out - mostly, and is now long once again. We wish you strength and healing during your treatments. We send our love to you.
—Cousins Judy and Robin,
June 1, 2015

Hi Jen, Just heard about your journal and read all the way back through. What a fast and scary journey you reveal. You can now hear us Wolinskys cheering for you. Keep on!
—Hugs from Cary, Babs, Yari and
Amber, June 1, 2015

Jen, I too am in awe of all the talent you have both in athletics and writing. I hope you are saving these meaningful poems and thoughts that will be comforting to others. We have great plans for your writing career.
—Helaine, June 1, 2015

THE SUN IS FINALLY OUT and I watched it fill up our living room from my favorite spot, the bathroom. Apparently, the Allopurinol and Senna are working as everything I eat, drink, breath seems to come right back out of me. Everyone comments on how skinny I am looking and that I need to eat more. Well, I can assure you, I am eating. My body just doesn't want to absorb anything!

I woke up with intentions to climb with Sandor. I promised him a Sandor day, as soon as I could walk on my ankle and leave the toilet. So far, I was not off to a good start. To top it off, I ran my hand through my hair and it came out full of grey, yellow, and brown strands. Right on time. I guess the doctors weren't joking. I didn't defy chemo.

Finally, forty- five minutes later, I was ready to attempt to leave and go play. I changed into my climbing clothes leaving more strands of hair on my pajama top. I packed my climbing gear, a baguette, salami and cheese. I threw on my hat, in case I should go bald for the drive to Cecil Rock, Sandor's favorite climbing spot. He led the first route so I could see how my ankle felt.

I led the second and we both led the next three. He was out of climbing shape, but daring and has no fear. I was in great climbing shape, but scared. It didn't help that if I scratched my head or took off my sunglasses, pieces of hair would fall to the ground. Climbing is the one sport that can usually channel my thoughts, force me to be in the moment, and forget about all else. Today, it was not working.

I kept trying to remind myself that my hair should be the least of my worries. It means that I am getting better. Unfortunately, it seems like a bit of a catch 22. Really, how can going bald mean that your state of health is improving! What I should be worried about is my second chemo coming up and not falling, as right now that could be catastrophic, NOT my hair!

The biopsy that I was so worried about was more important than losing my hair and it came out showing what we assumed. It showed that my indolent B cells had transformed in some areas to diffuse large B cells. This is not good, but it is not the worst. It just confirmed that we were correct in choosing the more aggressive treatment. But why have they not figured out this hair thing!

I went between smiling and laughing to getting teary eyes and crying. We would cheer each other on and then hold each other in between pitches. I am sure the climbers next to use thought we were crazy. After all, it just looked like I had a sprained ankle. One girl said she aspired to be me in the future. I told her thanks. If she only knew!

FALLING

I sleep and wake up to hair on my pillow
Brush it in the morning and it falls out
I put it in a ponytail and am scared to remove the elastic
My sunglasses collect strands as I remove them from my head
My scalp is flakey and my hair feels synthetic
Like the hair on a childhood doll
It does not feel connected to my body and hangs limply on my head
I wear a hat to block the sun
It too collects pieces of hair and I wonder what I look like
It blows in the wind as I climb
I worry the wind will take my hair with it
I dare not touch it and maybe it will last another day
I am scared to shower
Will I come out bald
Should I use shampoo
Or just put it off a few days
I need a clipper
But do I wait Or do it now
How
I like my hair
I don't want to lose it
But I don't want it to fall out
I want to be in control
But I don't
Want to be
Bald

PETSCAN

A hot liquid runs through my veins
I enter into a tunnel to be scanned
It buzzes and reads my heart, my lungs, my kidneys, my cells
Tomorrow the scans will come back and Dr.Alec will read them to me
My body is black with florescent yellow nodules all over my stomach, my butt,
*   and some on my lungs*
My heart works, my kidneys work, but my white blood cells are replicating too fast
And they are dangerous and are taking over my insides
The scan is like a piece of art lit up and tinted with action
It reads where there is metabolic activity
There are places where it should occur
Arteries need sugar to function; hearts, lungs, kidneys
But there are places where it should not occur
White blood cells do not need sugar as they do not need to replicate
And if they are not blocked then they will take over and
Squeeze the functioning arteries that I need to exist
White blood cells cannot be stopped by diet or exercise
They cannot be stopped by over the counter drugs, massages, or acupuncture
And they hurt as they shoot electricity up my spine and down my leg
They pinch my sciatic nerve and squeeze my intestines
The only option to eradicate them is chemotherapy
It will crush them and turn them to debris like a bomb
It will attack them and shatter them so they won't come back
But I will suffer and feel poisoned
I will lose my hair
But the pain will go away
And the cells will disappear
And hopefully
I will
Live

STILL NOT BALD

June 1, 2015

I MUST REALLY HAVE A LOT of hair, because I am pulling it out by the handful and I still look fairly normal. I think I am clogging the drains and shedding all over the sheets. At least, I am getting rid of all my grey. Oh, well! I'm going to keep it as long as I can. I can't bring myself to buzz it even though we bought clippers the other day.

I have to say one more thank you to everyone for your wonderfulness. I mentioned needing work on Facebook and have had a gazillion calls. I mentioned only being able to eat bread and popsicles and came home to homemade Challah from Jeffers and a freezer full of popsicles from Sandor. A bunch of friends called offering to go grocery shopping for me.

I also came home to letters from cousins and their kids (Marissa) with the sweetest messages. I got ginger candy from a mystery person (anyone??) and an orchid from my wonderful kindergarten class and their teacher, Mrs. Lammers. Thank you everyone! And thanks to the VAC, my health club, that has kept me sane. I do not know how I would have survived this last month without you!

It is amazing how everyone pulls through in times of need. It just goes to show what we are made of and capable of. It is too bad so many people in the world are fighting when really it is so easy to be kind to one another. Just a few words or simple gestures mean so much and go such a long way. I am reminded how lucky I am every day despite my circumstances.

With that being said, I am living every day to its fullest. Sandor would say too full. I am always anticipating being bald and sick again and don't want to waste a moment. It has made me play hard, even with my swollen ankle. I fit in a short ride today and am climbing before work tomorrow. I applied for a bunch more jobs today and babysat this afternoon for the cutest kid ever (besides Maggie, my niece, of course)!

Everyone thinks I am crazy, but I am much happier when I am busy. I don't like sitting and chilling out. I know that's what I should be doing. Sandor has been trying to teach me the art of chilling since he met me. But, it is just not me. I will chill next week, as I will have no choice, but not now.

Until Monday, play on, hair or no hair!

I DID IT!

June 3, 2015

COMMENTS

Beautiful, Jen! You are so brave! Even in a situation where you felt powerless you took some of that back. I am sure you look beautiful—the new normal is strange I am sure but this is a season. Looking forward to celebrating the next season for you on the other side of all of this! Keep going!
    —Lisa, June 5, 2015

Jen, I wake up every morning and open my email to see if you have written. You did it! You are brave and strong and amazing! Life gives us gifts that do not come with a bow... You are one of them!!! Thank you letting me be close. See you soon in Vail.
    —Edith, June 4, 2015

I did appreciate, however, how nice it was to not have to spend any time washing/drying/fussing with my hair—more than that, there was a freedom that I came to value in being without hair—at least for a while. You are more exposed, you do need to think about who you are without hair and, like you said you're not your hair. You are so, so much more and what you have is richer and deeper than anything hair will ever give you. We just think you're great. As always thank you for sharing so much with us—it means a great deal.
    —Sam, June 4, 2015

I DID IT. It might have been one of the hardest things that I have ever done in my life, but it is done. It got to the point when I had no choice. I woke up to piles of hair on my pillow. I brushed my hair and chunks came out. I went to ride and piles of hair stuck to my helmet and pulled out when I took my sunglasses off.

I kept trying to make it last another day. If I don't touch it, it will stay on my head. If I don't shower or brush it, it won't fall out. I need just one more day to go out with my friends and feel normal! Then it got to the point that I was disgusted by my own self. I was sick of being scared to touch my hair or shake it. I decided I would rather shave it than walk around with chunks of it missing.

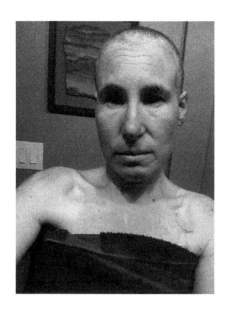

Sandor bought the clippers, I brought the vacuum upstairs, and we went to work. He was patient and kind and actually did a pretty good job for a scientist. He is detailed and thorough and he cares, so I trusted him. First we cut it to an inch, then a half inch, a quarter inch, and then almost to an eighth. That's when I freaked and we decided to give it a day with a little fuzz. I watched my hair fall to the floor. All blond strands, brown strands, and the grey ones too.

We laughed, I cried, and then I felt free because it was done. No more thinking about it or deciding what day to do it. It was done. I tried on hats, wigs, turbans and decided they all itch and look silly. I will probably wear a wig initially just to avoid comments, but eventually I think I'll go Demi Moore style. I might not look like her, but it is a lot more comfortable than wearing a wig.

I did get to ride my bike before babysitting and chopping off my hair today. I got to snap a few more memories of me with hair. I had a good day with a good group of friends. They helped me to remember I am who I am, hair or no hair. Losing hair is such a minor side effect in the scheme of the pain from the cancer and the chemo treatments, yet it is amazing how it feels just as painful if not more painful.

How you style your hair, color it, wear it is a part of your identity. When it is gone you feel like you are losing a part of you. You also feel naked and like you are making it clear to everyone that you are sick. You can't hide from the disease anymore. So you have to hang tough and not think about what others will think. You have to prepare to smile back at them and make the conversation light, so it doesn't seem so heavy, even though it is.

Not ready to put up a picture yet.

FIRST
EXCURSIONS
WITH A BUZZ

June 5, 2015

COMMENTS

This is a great post, Jen. I am sure the hair affects you way more than others. Excited to see you tomorrow, and don't worry about having to look good for me! I like you the way you are, hair or not.
        —Rachel, June 5, 2015

Hi Jen, I am inspired by your amazing weekend. Hoping the week goes as well as can be. I love to see that competitive side of you come out. Thinking of you. Big hug,
        —Nate, June 8, 2015

You are indomitable! Wonder where it comes from? Love YA!
        —Mom and Dad, June 5, 2015

YOU DON'T REALIZE how much your hair keeps you warm until you don't have any. Last night, I had to get up and put a hat on in the middle of the night. Then I took a hot bath, just to warm up, and wore my hoodie while cooking breakfast. Now, I see why all the patrollers on the mountain grow beards in the winter time. A cheap form of insulation.

It felt weird to need such a small amount of shampoo and NO conditioner! I barely even had to towel dry my hair and I obviously didn't have to brush it. I couldn't stop running my hand through it and laughed as I realized I had been wearing an elastic hairband on my wrist all day. Probably won't need those for a while.

Sandor and I had plans to climb at 9:30 with some friends and it hit me, I had to make some decisions about what to do with my head, both fashion wise and health wise. Do I put on a wig or just be straight open and shock everyone? Do I wear a winter hat because I am so cold or a cute little baseball cap that will keep me warm and be fashionable? How do I cover up my head when I climb so I don't get sunburnt or too hot?

These are questions I never thought I would have to consider. I decided to bring it all. After about five minutes in the wig, I wanted to rip it off my head. I am obviously missing something that should go underneath it, because it was unbearable. It itched, it made my head feel like it was on fire, and it moved every time I turned my neck. Margaret reminded me models are probably not comfortable in half of the outfits they wear. I reminded her, that is why I am a hippie climber and not a model.

After stripping off the wig and putting on my winter beanie for the car ride, I decided to wear my cap up to the climb and then change to this ugly, but comfortable, turban from the cancer center.. A whole new section of wardrobe to coordinate, HATS! Paige didn't say much about my head on the way to climb and I realized it affected me more than everyone else. I did get looks at the rock when I went to lead the route and other climbers saw that I had no hair.

It is funny. People are automatically nice to you when you look sick, but are not sure what to say, whether to help, or just let you do your thing. Especially, since I was climbing perfectly fine. You almost want to relieve them of their curiosity, but then you think, do you really want to explain and answer the same questions again. This one guy even asked me if I wanted him to carry my rope down to the car. Guess cancer turns guys into gentlemen. Of course, I said, "No, but thanks."

Then I went to babysit. Although I know kids are resilient, I was a little bit afraid Zander would be scared of me. He smiled when I picked him up. He said where is mom and you look like a boy. I had my khaki hat on as I have been trying to match my hat to my belt. I suppose that between the camouflage and lack of hair, Zander's observation was a good one. I smiled and said, "Great, then I guess we look alike."

We spent most of the afternoon moving stuffed animals from his room to the guest room and then back to his room. The culminating event was an attempt to fit them all into a bed stand with one little drawer. An impossible feat, but not to a two-year old. The whole time I thought, how great to be so unbiased and easily entertained. Such simple satisfaction!

The big challenge came for me at night when I had to decide how to go out in public to meet an old friend who was in town. In Vail, it is the Go Pro Games free concert night and most likely I would know many people there. I didn't want to be the center of attention or have to explain my situation to everyone, yet I hate that wig. So, I decided to try the more natural colored one, rather than the Christie Brinkley, obviously not me, wig. Although, it was tempting!

It worked well as everyone complimented me on my haircut and told me I looked great. Someone even said, you look so healthy, what's your secret? Cancer, I thought, but didn't say it out loud. As great as it was to pull it off, is as awful as it felt on my bare head. After a slice of pizza at Vendettas and a good hour of socializing at the concert, hugging lots of wonderful, caring friends, but explaining my story too many times, I needed to get the wig off!

It itched like crazy and the top part cut into my ears while the bangs fell into my face and made my nose itch. As OK as I look and feel, I still am constantly reminded that I am sick. I headed to the car as fast as I could, tempted to just rip it off while walking down the street. In the future, I would have to figure out what to wear to make the wig more bearable or become O.K. with being bald.

It is amazing how in a few months socializing has taken on a new form. I socialize, but am always half preoccupied with being sick. It doesn't help that lately a normal night out has not started off with; "How are you?" "Work?" "The kids?" Instead it's, "How are you feeling?" "What has it been like?" "How did you find out?" "Maybe, I have cancer too?"

It is not bad or good, it just is. I would be offended if people didn't ask or care and it is still new. Plus it is on my mind. While everyone else is working, I am dealing with chemo so it is what I know right now. I assume at some point; it will become the new norm. Being bald will just become a part of the day and everyone will ask how I am and then move on to the typical small talk. At some point, I will be able to forget about my life for a little bit and enjoy the moment.

Meanwhile, I am going to call my bald friends and ask them for hat advice!

ANOTHER GREAT DAY

June 7, 201

I DON'T WANT THE GOOD DAYS to end! I am getting to see all my favorite people and I feel great! This is a tease! I am totally better and don't want to be knocked down again on Monday! I keep thinking the doctors made a mistake or are going to see how positively I respond to the chemo and tell me I don't need any more treatments. Why would you make someone sick if they are doing just fine?!

I had a wonderful last few days. You really learn to appreciate every moment when you know the moments are limited and will end soon. All the little things that you normally worry about or that would bug you go away because you are so happy to just be alive. I unloaded and planted annuals on Friday, something that would just be typical, but that right now made my day. Then, I was taken to dinner by more great friends and even had a Margarita.

Today, I rode up Battle Mountain in the sun and down in the snow. I loved every minute of it. I got to have lunch with a good friend I hadn't seen in forever and she brought me more ginger. Ginger!! Thanks, Rach! Then to top it off, I got to run the timing for the bouldering competition at the Go Pro Games and I didn't ruin the event. Being a computer dummy, I was worried because the guy in charge had a heavy French accent and I couldn't understand what he wanted me to do. So I just prayed, and it worked! I clicked the right buttons at the right time and everyone got their four minutes to win. Thanks, Larry for giving me front row seats!

G. Love ended the night with some new songs and his good old hit, "Special Sauce." He didn't recognize me, but I waved to him. We went to highschool together. I wore my wig, talked about biking, climbing, and food. I felt totally normal. I even got compliments on my blond hair and looking skinny. I wasn't sure if people thought I just lost weight and dyed my hair or if they knew. Either way it was nice to be complimented.

I have even been debating whether to compete in the time trial tomorrow. I feel that good, but am spoiled and am not sure I want to get up that early because it is COLD! I've been riding so well that I was thinking the drugs I have been taking have steroids in them, but I don't think so. I think it is that you go from feeling so bad to feeling better, and that better feels magnificent because the bad is so bad. It also probably helps that I am 15 pounds lighter and eating ice cream every night.

It would be cool to win a race on the day before chemo, but it would also be nice to sleep in. Gotta enjoy feeling good while I can. We'll see what the weather looks like in the morning

ROUND TWO DONE!

June 8, 2015

I SAT DOWN TO WRITE this journal entry three times and am just now formulating a sentence. The first time, I had to take a nap. The second time, I had to take a walk that I didn't even complete and the third time, I decided to eat ice cream instead. Can you say not productive! I guess the day of chemo I will not be getting much done. I guess the term chemo fog exists for a reason.

They say there is not necessarily medical proof that your brain changes with chemo, but between the chemicals and the mental stress patients tend to have trouble focusing the week of treatment. This is extra rough if you're me and already have trouble focusing. Physically, I was prepared for the worst as always. I came in a little less anxious than the last time, but nervous to have chemicals again after feeling so good last week.

My Neutrophil count was borderline so that made me a little bit nervous, but the second Leesa finished flushing my port with saline, friends arrived to visit me. I wasn't sure if company would be good or not, but it turned out that it made the day go by so much faster! Every time someone left, someone else came in. I brought cards, magazines, popsicles. Instead, I ended up smiling as my friends entertained me with stories about their week, work, their lives. What a great distraction and chance to catch up with my amazing friends. Thank you!

I made Sandor stop at Walmart on the way home so I could restock on bread. Then we took a short walk around the block. I feel like moving is so much better than sitting still and letting the chemicals slosh around. However, I wasn't moving very fast. I fell asleep immediately when we got back home. I have been attempting to write ever since I woke up. I have some physical issues that are adding to the distractions.

My body aches a bit and I am on fire, but have the chills. The metal taste isn't super strong yet, but I have a salty taste on my lips. I have a little headache. I'd say all in all, it felt much easier than the first round. "Knock on Wood." I have less cells to kill and therefore less debris to get rid of. I plan to work and babysit tomorrow, knowing that I probably am not going to want to ride my bike or go climbing. I figure if I can't play, I should try to work. In general, I need to work.

We'll see how tomorrow goes. Two down, four to go!! I am 33% done!

DAY AFTER CHEMO 2

June 9, 2015

I rode my bike to work at the garden today, babysat, and then biked Berry Creek! It was at a record slow pace and I felt tired, sore, and nauseous, but I did it. I planned on feeling sick and sleeping all day, but decided staying in bed would make me feel worse than being occupied. I am exhausted right now, but wouldn't have done it any other way.

I've decided I do believe in mind over matter. I am prepared for the fight to get harder, as I know that chemo has a cumulative effect. I also believe I can choose to feel sick and sorry for myself or choose to keep life as normal as possible, within reason. I figure if I can bike Berry Creek today, I will still be able to bike on my last treatment. It might just be to East Vail and back, but it will be something.

As awful as chemo is, the process is mentally so much better than the anticipation. Not knowing what you have, how you will react, what the prognosis will be is the worst. Living, knowing this is just the start of the battle is hard, but at least the healing has started and I have two down and four to go.

My friends probably dug more holes at work than I did today. Other babysitters were probably more fun than me and everyone rode faster than I did, but I was out there! Now, I am going to sleep. Thank goodness!

SICK OF EATING

June 13, 2015

I am finding that between chemo and gardening, my life is busier than ever. Over the past summers, I have worked, played, and worked some more. Now I work, play, and have to fit in time to be sick! Mom and Dad you are amazing! I can't imagine having chemo Monday, working Tuesday, and coming home and having to cook and take care of anyone or anything except myself. I am so selfish. I don't know how you did it, and kudos to those who have been sick and done it! Wow!

This week's treatment was easier than the first. I would not say that it was pain free or without side effects, but   they were less severe. I believe that I had so many cancer cells the first round, that all the debris from the chemicals made it a really rough treatment. It didn't help that I had to go to Denver for a biopsy the next day. This round I felt like I had the flu; chills, aches, fatigue, stomach issues, but I gardened and babysat most of the week and even did a second bike ride on Friday. It is the taste of the chemicals that is so awful!

The two challenges for me have been what to eat and getting adjusted to my lack of hair. Both have left me puzzled. I am not sure what to put in my body or what to wear on my head. I guess we all have decisions to make, but these are not ones that I thought I would have to deal with in my life- time. I have watched videos on head wraps and read books and articles galore on food. I am slowly figuring out what will go in and stay in and how to keep the scarf from falling off. I will probably get it down by round six, but in the meanwhile, the battle has been rough.

Just like round one, I sleep, eat, and smell the chemicals. I am hungry, but nothing is appealing, and if it is, it isn't a minute later. Sandor went out

43

and bought me a half-pound of salami, excited I craved something and it is still in the fridge. I bought bags of sucker candies and they make me sick just looking at them. However, if I don't have something in my mouth at all times, I start to taste the metal. Cheeze-Its have worked well, along with PB&J, vanilla ice cream, and salt and vinegar potato chips. I know that sounds like a great diet to most, but I am sick of eating. When those are your choices in food, they don't always leave you feeling so great!

As far as the hair goes, I am getting adjusted. It is way easier! I jump out of the shower and my hair is dry. No more shampoo, conditioner, or hair ties. However, I have one more item of clothing to coordinate and I am not a fashion person, if you hadn't guessed. I am used to throwing on my ski cap and leaving. Now I have to find a hat for under my bike helmet, for climbing, for gardening, and then bring a wig if I plan to go out in public and don't want to be questioned. It is a lot to envision before work!

I have surprisingly, gotten a lot of compliments the few times I have gone out. I get, "You look so skinny. When did you go blond? Your hair has been styled so perfectly lately! You eat so much how do you stay in such good shape?" The best was, "You look so healthy! What is your secret?" I am always tempted to say cancer and the hair is fake, but I guess I might as well go with the compliments if they are being given. I also discovered that there are things to wear under the wig so you don't itch your scalp off. Duh!

Even though I can't eat properly and I did not want to lose my hair, I decided I would have some fun with all the hats and scarves I have been sent. I felt like a kid again trying them all on until I remembered that I am forty and have cancer. I decided to forget about all that and here is what I came up with. You'll have to let me know which look you like the best. Until then, enjoy that you can taste what you eat and that you don't have to coordinate your head with your outfit!

I want to thank everyone once again as I have come home to lemon bars, sunflowers, beach hats, challah, sunglasses, bath bubbles, sunscreen, banana cream pie, Lemonheads, gift certificates, blankets. You name it, someone has thought of it! I am overwhelmed with the letters, calls, and texts. I only hope I am getting to each one of you to thank you. If not please know how grateful I am. Sandor is grateful too. I love all the gifts, but knowing that you care means so much to me. I am humbled and hope I can do the same in return. I love you guys!

EMBARRASSMENT AND EVERYDAY OBSTACLES

June 16, 2015

MY DAY YESTERDAY was a page from a book, Cancer Made Me Shallower, specifically the chapter, Embarrassment and Everyday Obstacles. That was the theme that started in the morning and continued throughout my day. It came up at breakfast, work, during my bike ride, and again at dinner.
I suppose it is something I am going to have to deal with throughout this process. Do I suck it up or tell everyone I know what is going on. Let me further explain this by giving you an outline of my daily schedule with the stream of thoughts that are going through my mind. I am aware that most people are compassionate and are thinking about other things, not me. However, in my brain, this is how it goes….

2:00 a.m. Gotta' pee! Thirsty!!

4:00 Gotta' pee again! Damn! Don't let it sit in you, get the poison out! Man, am I thirsty! Pepsi, that will make the bad taste go away. Really you should try to sleep a little bit more. You could do Rosetta Stone. No, you should sleep!

6:30 Gotta' pee! Thirsty, so thirsty! Time to get up. Not hungry, but gotta' eat so I have two hours before taking my drugs, try to take a dump, and pack hats and wigs to garden, bike, and go out. Eggs, no toast, nothing looks good. Cereal! Plain, no milk.

7:30 Going to garden armed with toilet paper and prayers that I don't have to go. How will I sneak out and hide for that long? What if there are no trees? I need a job with a bathroom! Please stomach, cooperate! Ohhh, electric pains in my body again! Suck it up!

9:00 My body temperature must be 20 degrees hotter than it was before chemo. That is OK. They said this might happen. Wear sunscreen and keep your long sleeve shirt on no matter what! At least there are some clouds today and I'm just planting Marigolds and Snaps. Easy! Sweating like crazy! How embarrassing! Bad taste in my mouth!

10:30 Still have to go. Oh, really have to now! Better find a tree. Hope none of the crew is nearby. What if the family is in their house? What if the family across the yard is in their house? Where should I hide? Dang!

12:00 Made it till lunch. Now I can go find a gas station and get sick again. I guess I should buy something. There must be a soda or juice that will make this taste go away. So glad the gas station was close by. Thank goodness! That was a close call! It is tiring to have to work around being sick.

3:00 Meeting friends to ride. Will I make it? What if I feel sick on the trail? Doing good. Wow, second lap and still OK. Third lap, Wow, I'm a rock star. Fourth lap, not feeling so good. Uh Oh, getting nauseous. Need a tree. Oh,

man, wish I had TP. Got a sock? Yuk! Keep riding everyone, I'll be OK.
I hope! Dang it, how embarrassing!

5:40 Feeling really sick need to throw up. Stomach going crazy. What if
I can't ride back. Getting sick. Hope no one can see me bald and vomiting.
Catch your breath and try to ride back to the car. It is not that far. You can
do it!

6:00 Driving fast, need to get home. Should I stop at the gas station? Will
I make it to the house? I would rather be in my house than at the gas station
again. What hat do I wear into the gas station? Shit, I forgot my hat! Making
it to the house. Made it!

6:30 Been in the bathroom for half an hour now. Might as well fricken'
move in

7:30 Gonna go out as I have been planning all week. Going to pizza. Do I wear a
hat? A wig? What if I get sick there too? If I don't eat will people think I am weird?
What if my hat moves my wig and everyone laughs? Do I even want to go out?

8:00 Lots of people at the bar. Do they know? Can they tell I am faking it?
Do they care? Probably not at all. How selfish of you to think that everyone
is thinking about you. I am sure they have plenty of other things to think
about. You are the only one that knows you have cancer and that your hair is
fake. Should I drink? Eat pizza? Will it taste good or like metal? Will it stay in
me? 'A slice of pizza and a rum and coke please!' Yuk to both! Focus on the
conversation, not on you. Focus!

11:00 Not a bad night. Didn't get sick at Vendettas. Now the big question
whether to take a Senna or not? I don't want to be constipated, but I don't
want to have the runs. Not sure which is worse. Hmmm...body tired, brain
tired, going to bed, then doing it all over again tomorrow.

Life used to be so easy! I suppose this will become routine. I will know which
hat to grab for what, which foods taste good and which do not, and whether
to take a Senna or not. Or, possibly it will be a puzzle that I have to figure
out. Either way, it is keeping me on my toes and is better than dying. It is just
an added challenge to the day. No dull moments. Hopefully, what
I find embarrassing, friends understand. If not, oh well! Life throws obstacles
at people. You can let them be barriers or tackle them even if it might be
extremely difficult.

Might have to take it a bit easier today!

STILL ALIVE

June 21, 2015

SORRY I HAVEN'T WRITTEN. I am still alive. Actually doing really well. So well, that I went camping and climbed all weekend. Last week was rough: a crown fell out, my dryer broke and my dishwasher flooded. I also worked a ton and fell asleep every time I planned to write. It was great to play and forget that I was sick and that my condo was falling apart.

A couple of updates. Last week a friend sent me Miracle Berries. They look like rose hips and are sour, but make your food taste sweet. Pretty cool! I also bought Dry Mouth toothpaste and mouthwash, as the little girl I babysit for suggested. Between the two, I was able to eat and camp and sleep through the night.

I actually got in a full week of work! The Marigolds are doing well and I even put some yellow Snapdragons in my garden. I have been taking one Senna instead of two and my stomach is feeling much better. The four-year-old I babysit for told me I look fine and not to worry my hair will grow back. The two-year-old little boy told me I look like a boy. Oh well, guess you can't please everyone.

I ordered a soft hat from my mom's friend in brown and black as wigs are too much work. I did get a beautiful wig from my mom's friend (thank you) that is light and comfortable, but it's white blond. I will try it on and post soon. I will keep it for a daring day! I also got pears and cheese which we ate at the base of the climb. Should have brought wine!

Back to this weekend, it was marvelous! Just what the doctor ordered. I have been scared to camp with my stomach issues, immune system, teeth falling out, but it was great! I forgot that I was a cancer patient. I climbed with a friend of mine, who is a guide, and we went nuts. We did ten pitches on Saturday and four on Sunday.

There was no sympathy only climbing and camping and eating. I felt normal. It didn't matter that I was bald or sick, I was just me!

I am back at home and happy to shower. I cleaned the house, the car, and me. I re-organized all the stuff that fell off the shelves that crumbled when the dryer broke. I watered my garden. I ate steak and Kasha. I got to hear about Sandor's weekend of being wined and dined by a friend of ours who writes reviews for local restaurants. I was jealous, but not that jealous. I love food, but I love hanging from ropes at high heights and sleeping under the stars.

My hands and toes are happily sore. It will be good to work tomorrow and give my body a break!

PHILOSOPHIZING

June 21, 2015

SO I AM FINDING that my diagnosis has made people think that I have this new wealth of knowledge about life and health care. Someone asked me about their father's heart condition and another friend wanted advice about her future. I wanted to respond, "I don't know. What should I do with mine?" I was asked why my runner friend was peeing blood and if 108 was a low white blood cell count. I was surprised that I did have the answers to some of these questions, but it's only because I live with Sandor, not because I have cancer. I have learned a lot about health, but I am still waiting to have some kind of earthmoving epiphany about life.

Everyone says you will come out of this a better person. You will have a new perspective on the world. Something good will come from all this suffering. What if this does not happen for me? What if I come out just how I was before? Is that so bad? What if all my life problems are still there when I complete chemo and I don't see any fireworks or have any new revelations? Does everyone come out changed? What if I change for the worse?

I have been trying to read deep books about life. I bought A New Earth by Eckhart Tolle, but ended up reading Rock and Ice instead. I went to yoga the other day, but couldn't stand on my head. Crow hurt my wrists, and when I tried to "Ommm" at the end of class I sneezed. Then I thought wearing my Buddha hat would make me look like the wise person I am supposed to be. Instead, the little boy I babysit for asked me why I was wearing a funny cloth on my head.

As much as I want to be wiser, I don't think you can race to acquire wisdom. I think it comes with experience and that you don't realize you are acquiring it. It just kind of happens. I am still at the beginning of this process. I am not sure what lessons I have learned so far and am not sure what lessons are to come. Meanwhile, I am getting good at making stories up and sounding enlightened.

I don't need yoga just a bunch of good lines. I already look Zen with my bald head and baggy clothes.

SOME SERIOUS QUESTIONS

June 24, 2015

TODAY WAS A BUSY BABYSITTING DAY full of all kinds of kid medical questions. I was amazed at their interest and wonderful perspective on how life works. I had to think hard to find creative ways to explain my situation in four- year- old terms and remind myself that their black and white responses do have some grey in the middle.

The questions began when I had to leave babysitting for an hour to go fix my crown that had fallen out due to chemo. Aviva looked up at me and said, "I didn't know that adults lose teeth too. Does the Tooth Fairy come for them?" Ella, Aviva's neighbor, proceeded to tell us that she had gotten ten dollars for her tooth because she is ten–years-old. I figured, I could get rich if my teeth keep falling out, but responded, "Sometimes adults do lose teeth and usually the Tooth Fairy only comes for kids." "I am sorry," said Aviva, "but it will be OK, we'll just eat lots of pudding."

When I returned from the dentist we decided to start a project clearing out all the "baby" books on her bookshelf and keeping only the books that four–year-olds would read. We came across a book of short stories that Aviva had been reading with a story about a woman who has Leukemia. Aviva asked me if the lady in the story also ate a lot of Jolly Ranchers. I said, "Probably if they had them back then." She asked, "Do all the medicines I take require eating candy and do lollipops work?" I said, "All of my medicines make me thirsty and leave a bad taste in my mouth so that is why I always have hard candies." I saw her eyeing my bag and realized why the question had come up. She chose the red, I chose the blue and we sucked on them while we put

The Three Little Bears in the give -away pile and Little Miss Ladybug on the keep shelf.

Around 3 p.m. I helped Aviva change into her too big Tae Kwan Do outfit. We wrapped the belt around her waist three times. We went to pick up Zander at Montessori and then headed to the Tae Kwan Do studio. Little Zander sat mesmerized as the three students, all in too big outfits, kicked in the air and yelled, "Yah,Yah". He didn't move while they, "Yes, ma'amed," bowed, and shook hands. "Do you want to do that when you get older?" I asked. "Yes ma'am," he responded. We dropped Zander off at his house and took a quick tour of his excavator trucks, as promised, even though Mom and Dad were already home.

On the way back to West Vail, Aviva asked, "How many medicines do you have to take?" I realized every time I ate a sucker candy; a medical question would come up. "On the weeks that I am really sick so many that I can't count, but none this week!" "That is OK, I had the croup once and the medicine made me all better. If you just follow what the doctor tells you, you will get better too and all the white dots will go away."

Previously, I had explained that I had red cells and white cells in me and that the white cells were taking over. Every three weeks, I have to take medicine to stop them.

In her astute voice Aviva said, "You mean it is like a battle?"
"Yes, when they give me medicine it attacks the bad white cells and so I feel sick."
She said, "You mean like a war?"
"Yes, like a war."
" In the end who wins?"
" Me and the medicine, I hope."
" I think you'll win. Sometimes people go away forever you know."
" Yes," I said, " but I hope that I don't go away forever."
" Don't worry, if you do we will still have a birthday party for you, but we will have to sell your house."
" OK," I said."
" But, it is way better to lose your hair than to die."
" Yes, I agree."
" And when you get better you will get more hair and you won't have to eat Jolly Ranchers anymore."
 "Yes", I giggled. "I am glad I get to hang out with you because you always make me smile and feel better."
" You can stay at my house forever, if you want," she said.
" Thanks," I said, "I will think about that!"

ROUND THREE
(QUESTIONS FOR DOCTOR ALEC AND PRE-CHEMO BBQ)

June 29, 2015

I DO NOT KNOW, at this point, where my journal will go. However, it is my intention to help anyone who is going through what I am going through. Therefore, I would like to make sure I am adding any useful information along with my random stories and pictures. So here are the questions that I plan to ask the doctor at my next chemo treatment.

Can I have a dental cleaning while having chemo? X-rays? Do I need to take antibiotics before it?

Can I have an allergy shot? Allergy medicines? Can I take Aleve or only Tylenol?

Is it the Prednisone that is making me into a superhero? Pig? Any other ideas for dry mouth as I am parched all the time? Can I make plans to go away as soon as chemo ends?

Can I take allergy medicine? Claritin? Shots? Is Chemo brain proven or just hypothetical?

BBQ

I climbed eight routes in Rifle and rode Meadow Mountain and Vail. I am worked in a good way and ready to barbeque. Just ate two bratwursts, a chocolate chip cookie, ice cream and a Smirnoff Ice. I am feeling fat and happy. I have to eat a lot while everything tastes good, before chemo tomorrow. I am actually ready to rest for a few days. However, I could do without a visit to Shaw. Not sure chemo can be considered a rest day.

I think my mind and body go nuts with anticipation the day before treatment. I can't stop the adrenaline and I need to feed it with junk food! I even dream about chemo or should I say have nightmares about it. This week, in my dream, I came home from my treatment to a mansion decorated in velvet blue, where a hot bath awaited me, and flowers filled the room. Goblets of wine and grapes were set on a large glass table and my cousins and family were there fanning me off as I walked in. But, everything smelled and tasted like aluminum, my body reeked of chemicals, and the air smelled metallic.

Too bad I can't leave out the last part of the nightmare and just go with the mansion and the food. However, I do dream good dreams. Dreams of climbing in Greece, fresh cucumbers, and Tzatziki. Dreams of beaches with women handing out pineapples on a stick and papaya. Those dreams are not tinted with sickness. I also got to thoroughly enjoy my friends and chat with my family today. Molly and I took action photos while riding through the Aspens and Sarah and I hung from Limestone and ate Fajitas and Margaritas at Casa Mexico. Despite the nightmares, there has been goodness in every day.

I took a photo for a friend who has spread the word in the Vail community that I am sick. She has praised me with kind words and compliments that I do not deserve, but am honored to receive. I like the photo because it reminds me to slow down, get off my bike, look around, smell the flowers, and enjoy the journey. It is hard to remember that there are so many things to appreciate in life.

Tomorrow I will come armed with my questions, my good luck bead bracelet (thank you Louis), and my good BBQ memories. Mom, Dad, and Laur, I will bring my phone and answer it if you call. I am ready.

Bring on round three. Half way there, three more to go!

THE PROCESS

June 29, 2015

I AM SLOWLY LEARNING the process and the pattern, something the nurses and doctors know, but you must learn over time. The huge weight loss is at the start when you are first diagnosed and freaking out. Then you begin the chemo and gain ten pounds in liquid weight, even though you are still nervous and not eating because everything tastes so bad. You are tired, sore, and freaked out, but the pain from the cancer is going away.

Week two, you feel better, but then you're stressing out about your hair falling out. You're still bloated and everything tastes metallic, so eating is not appealing. Week three comes along and you want to eat everything because you are feeling good and food actually starts to taste normal again. You crave protein and don't care what people think about your eating habits.

Then you go for chemo Round Two. You are nervous, but less than the last time. You go through the same process except you have already lost your hair. You are self-conscious, but you know the nurses and they are wonderful and supportive. They complement you and still coddle you as they know the process is still new to you. You thank them with all of your might.

This time you eat non-stop. There is no fighting the Prednisone so you succumb to it. It makes you ravenous and thirsty and the doctors tell you to eat and gain weight. You realize the only way to make the chemical taste go away is to eat all the time, so you do. Ice cream, bread, chips, burgers, brats!

You ride and climb like a rock star because your cancer cells have decreased. You have residual Percocet and Prednisone in you. You are on a rampage because you know you are out again in a few weeks. You are feeling strong, hungry, and aggressive. You don't want to be knocked down again. You forget you are sick, until you look in the mirror.

Chemo Three and you go in heavier than before, but still skinnier than you have ever been. Everyone compliments you and says you are looking great. You know the nurses, the doctors, and the people who come in for chemo on Monday. You know the snacks you want on your table and are learning the timetable of your cocktails. You know when to pee and when to get ready to give out your name and birthday.

The rest is unknown, but I believe with each treatment you do become wiser, if you observe. Just like anything you do and learn. Like Bloom's Taxonomy, you analyze and then synthesize it all together. You begin to see how your body reacts to different chemicals, foods, and what you need to make the bad days better. Everyone is different so you can listen to their stories and advice, but you learn to live your reality. Hopefully, you learn to make it tolerable and maybe even wonderful on the days in between.

It is all a process. You must take the bad with the good and go with the flow. Predicting and planning are helpful, but only with tolerance and flexibility.

THE CYCLE

I am slowly learning how it works
Check my vitals 179/77 too high
118/58 that's more like it
Check my name birthdate and take my blood
Meet with Doctor Alec.
Ask him questions
Blood tests OK, white blood cell count borderline
Check my name, check my birthdate
Administer Aloxi over 45 minutes or half an hour
What do you choose?
Computerize before the Benadryl kicks in
Bladder full, gotta pee
The Aloxi is beeping
Time for Rituximab
Name and birthdate please
Another hour this time I will attempt to sleep
I am dry, thirsty
One sip and have to pee Urghhh
Two infusions of Vincristin
The red stuff
Get it out, don't let it sit
It is the one that tastes bad
Gotta pee red
Now for Oncovin or Adriamycin
The short bag
Drip, drip, drip
27.6ml 27.5ml 27.4ml
Beeeeeeeep
Gotta pee
Saline
Cyclophosphamide
Done

BUCKET LIST

July 1, 2015

SO, HOPEFULLY, I am not going to die, but chemo makes me re-evaluate what is important to me and what I want to do with my time. So, I am making a bucket list. We'll see how I follow through. I figure you try to do what you can and your bucket list changes as you change. This is what was in my head tonight.

1. Go to Alaska and catch a salmon
2. Visit Iceland and Scandinavia when there is sunlight
3. Come up with a business that pays me enough to work a 40-60 hour week with the weekends off and 4-6 weeks of vacation a year
4. Remodel my bathroom and kitchen
5. Live in one house instead of two
6. Donate or work with a cancer charity (First Descents, Round-Up River Ranch)
7. Go to South America or Costa Rica and learn Spanish
8. Make a cherry pie that actually looks like one
9. Learn not to sweat the small stuff
10. Sit on my back porch and read by the river without worrying about anything else that has to get done
11. Climb in Greece
12. Lead Castleton Tower
13. Ride in Crested Butte and Gooseberry Mesa
14. Maybe get married, but if not take a picture in a wedding dress
15. Be more decisive
16. Go pumpkin picking with Maggie
17. Go to the beach with my family
18. Go hang-gliding again
19. Grow an herb garden and have the tomatoes come out before it snows
20. Heli ski

I realize these are lofty goals. I wonder if a bucket list is necessary because just going climbing locally is a great treat after being sick. Taking the time to be with people that you enjoy and appreciate your surroundings is enough. Maybe it's even better than going to Heli ski in Alaska. Meanwhile, I will keep my list, but be OK if I get sidetracked, don't check everything off, or maybe accomplish something else unexpected that I didn't write down.

Just hanging out with Sandor, Leslie, and Claire was a real treat today, no activity or destination needed.

COMMENTS

How did I meet Jen? Well I can't say when, where or how.... But suddenly there she was, in my life and I couldn't be more grateful to have such an awesome friend. I think maybe it was ice climbing, now when I think about it. So darn strong and solid, I must admit I am secretly jealous of her strength and tenacity. She is a crusher!!! As for the bucket list.... Heck... It doesn't seem lofty. The land of the midnight sun.... Yep that's my home turf.... I think that one would be easy. Leading Castleton.... No worries, I will be more than happy to be following. I will even bring some frosty margs for summit celebration!!!
　　—Mia, July 2, 2015

I think your list is fantastic. I'd love to join you for SOME of your adventures. You made me think about what I would put on my bucket list. I'll probably never play the piano like Van Cliburn or win a swimming medal at the Olympics, but I can spend more time with my beautiful, brave, older daughter.
　　—Mom, July 2, 2015

MORE POEMS

July 4, 2015

I MADE IT THROUGH ROUND THREE, but am more tired than I was after the last few treatments. I just can't seem to recover after work or a ride and need to sleep. My body aches like I have the flu, but if I keep busy I forget about it. Oh well, I guess that is how it goes. I have been doing pretty well so far. A little rest will probably do me some good.

So, while everyone else was out partying for the Fourth, we watched the Grateful Dead live from Chicago. I think this was Sandor's dream 4th of July. I have to admit that as much as it was not my vision of the night, I did dance to "Bertha" and sing "Scarlet Begonias" along with Weir. I think I might even have a better voice than he does even if I look more like a skinhead than a hippie. Sandor made fun of all the kids in the audience who he said can't be real Deadheads as they weren't even alive when the Dead were around. I had to remind him, I wasn't either.

I am hoping to have more energy today. I have big plans to climb and then go to a picnic. I have been leaving time in the middle of the day to take a nap. I think it might be time to take advantage of the free acupuncture and massage they offer at the cancer center. I have always wanted to get pampered, but when you have the option, it is hard to find the time. I thought I would be bored and depressed, but instead I am busy and stressed. I agree with the many people who have said to me that I need to learn how to rest.

Here are my few new poems. I spent most of the week not being able to get the chemical Oncovin out of my head. I tasted it, I smelled it, and every time cancer or the medical center came up, it made me feel ill. So, I wrote a poem about it.

ONCOVIN
*It is light
Oncovin, Oncovin
The sun is high
Oncovin, Oncovin
Snip back the Iris
Oncovin, Oncovin
Begonias are dead
Oncovin, Oncovin
Blue Lobelia too
Marigolds are still fighting
Oncovin,
Oncovin
Lupine is in bloom
Oncovin, Oncovin
Hyssop is too tall
Oncovin, Oncovin*

Lavender has spread
Oncovin, Oncovin
The weeds are gone
Oncovin, Oncovin
It is dark
The sun is low
Oncovin

Now, I get to be a little more Dr. Suess like. I know I am not a poet but it is fun to rhyme and a great way to pass time when I can't sleep at night.

CANCER SCHMANCER

Please no more chemo, I don't want anymore,
Let's kick its butt right out the door.
Looking at liquid makes me feel sick.
Thinking of Shaw does not do the trick.
My body aches and I have to poop
My head hurts and my teeth feel like goop.
The skin on my hands hurt, and my lips taste like glue,
I am constantly tired but wide awake too!
It is hard to think and I feel out of wack,
My fingers tingle and so does my back.

Biking is good and rock climbing too,
They help me forget all that I'm going through.
Peanut butter, coke, ice cream, and pickles are good,
Everything else I eat just tastes like wood.
Hot baths help and mint tea too,
I am halfway done and ready to be through.
Please make it end soon and go away for good.
Surely I deserve it, surely it should.
But if it should not, I will put up a fight
And kick cancer's ass with all of my might!

So to all of you out there who are sick too,
Chemo sucks and will make you feel blue.
Eat what you want and take care of you,
Before you know it you will be on round two.
Pamper yourself and smile a lot,
Remember what is important and what is not.
To you and to me lots of good luck and love,
We will show cancer what we are made of!

MORTALITY

July 8, 2015

MY VIEW OF MORTALITY has changed since my diagnosis. Having been faced with the possibility of dying, I realize that it is possible and is an inevitable part of living. I know it is trite to say that everyone will die at some point, but it is true. Today I was surrounded by wonderful people celebrating the life of a wonderful person who died too young. It was a day full of tears, but a day full of celebration and good memories.

It is funny how the silly moments stick in your mind; Benji dropping paint on me from his ladder while I gardened below him, riding Monarch Pass in a storm, and my struggling up Squid Kid and then watching Benji dance right up like a piece of cake. As his friends rode Village to Village (His favorite trail) and shared Benji stories, it felt like he was with us. We hugged in the rain as we spread his ashes at Lighter Point and Shade Tree Grove. We shivered through the puddles as the sky let loose and continued to complete the loop, hoping to see Benji pass us on the way down.

While everyone cried, I was thinking this will happen to me at some point. I hope I will fight cancer and win, but if I were to die, it would be OK. I would be more upset for everyone else as I am doing what I love to do. I am riding, climbing, and surrounding myself with good friends, just as Benji did. I am trying to enjoy every day and appreciate all that the world brings my way. I believe that Benji did that. He rode, he climbed, he laughed and he loved.

Obstacles in life that stressed me out before chemo do not seem as daunting anymore. Life is hard, but you can think about all the awful things that could happen, the what-if-this or what-if-that, but then you will never really live life to the fullest. I like that my doctor has not told me what will happen or how I will feel. Partially, I think, he does not know and partially he wants to let this be my journey. This gives me the ability to choose how I want to feel without worrying or having pre-conceived notions. It forces me to take it as it comes.

That is how I feel about Benji's life. I wish he was here, but I am glad he was and always will be a part of my world. I do not want cancer, but it is a part of my life. I can choose to be sick or choose to make the best of it. I can choose to mourn Benji's death or choose to celebrate his life. Maybe, sometimes, you have to choose to do a little bit of both. That is what we did today.

Meanwhile, I do have to say it was nice to have everyone offer me warm clothes and get first dibs on the hot shower, even though it was not necessary. Thank you and thank you Benji for bringing such a great crew of people together.

CHEMO BRAIN OR JUST ME?

July 10, 2015

I HAVE BEEN DENYING that there is such a thing called chemo brain. Dr. E. described it as "a mental fog that has scientific proof to exist," but I find that I have always fit that category. People are constantly sharing the list of dumb things that I've done over the course of my life which makes it hard to decipher if my recent mistakes are due to chemo or just being me. I have always been known for my funny stories and the circumstances that I tend to get myself in. I do think that they have been increasing in number and concentration.

I have been fairly calm about my recent faux pas. I just don't have the fight in me to care. However, the same friend has been with me through each incident and I think she is a bit more worried than me. She has become a firm believer that there is some truth in the theory that the chemicals are messing with my mind. I will share with you a few pre-chemo examples and then a larger group of post chemo examples and let you decide for yourself whether chemo brain exists or not.

Now let me say that my nickname has been Amelia Bedelia for most of my life. I take things literally and tend to have a bit of blond in me despite my lack of hair. I am OK with this and have learned to accept it and forgive myself for all of the items that I have lost and broken or things I've forgotten to do. I try my best to make lists and double check my actions, but inevitably things just go wrong. I have decided to punish myself for a short while and then let it go. However, lately some of my mistakes are causing other people problems.

I am going to start with some pre-chemo Jen stories that you might have heard, but will make you laugh again. My favorite, told often by my mom, is the time she gave me quarters to feed the fish in the pond. She expected me to go buy fish food from the dispenser but, instead I fed the quarters to the fish. Another good one was when my friend, Tammy, asked me to grab a jacket off a rack for her at a ski shop. I grabbed it and proceeded to knock over the entire rack which had a domino effect so in turn knocked over all the racks on one side of the store. A final Jen story is that I left my condo door unlocked one night and found some random person sleeping on my couch the next morning. These stories and more have trailed me all of my life blurring the line between chemicals and just Jen.

Post diagnosis, I have more stories. These will make you laugh, but might also make you cry. For example, in the last two months I have run off a trail that I jog all the time and fallen into the creek, left my keys in my ignition overnight, walked out of the cancer center after an appointment to find that I left my car doors wide open, and gotten my shoe lace caught in the escalator at the gym causing me to plummet down 10 metal steps face first. I have sprained my ankle while watching a friend climb, left the oven on overnight, and bought the same grocery list twice in one day.

To top it off, yesterday I drove over a huge rock at a property that I have been working at and got stuck teeter-tottering on top of it. I didn't have cell service, so I jumped out of the car, which was no longer touching the ground, and walked about a half a mile to get service. Meanwhile, I didn't know that the owners of the house were at home. They started a phone chain to find the poor cancer patient who had abandoned her car and wandered off.

It is great that everyone has so much sympathy for me, but quite possibly, it's too much! If I was a kid at school, I would be milking it, doing everything wrong, but as an adult I am causing unnecessary drama. I was Amelia Bedelia before cancer and now I am Amelia Bedelia on Prednisone. Kelli, my close friend and boss, has somehow been involved in each event. Initially, she said, "Oh, it is just you Jen!" After the last incident, when a co-worker said his sister had cancer and he thinks the chemicals affected her ability to focus, Kelli just grinned and looked at me.

As you can see there is a blurred line between the incidents at hand and just Jen occurrences. I guess it would make sense that I would be in a fog as they are putting two liters of cocktails in me every few Mondays. I would still rather not believe in the chemo brain theory. I think believing in it will make everything worse. Meanwhile, I am hoping not to provide any more entertainment for the gardening crew for a while. But, if I do, Jen incident or not, at least I have an excuse!

BOOKS, MOVIES, AND COOKING LIGHT

July 12, 2015

I AM OVERWHELMED by all that I have not gotten done since becoming sick. On D-day I was handed magazines, movies, books, yarn to knit, and Cooking Light. Most of these I have barely touched. I feel like I have had less down time and have been busier than I have ever been before. I am working more hours to make up for my pay cut. I am trying to be active on the days I feel well and I am having to plan on being sick every few Mondays and Tuesdays. I am too sick to read, cook (bluhhh), or knit. And on top of it, I have made writing and spending more time with friends, a priority. The magazines are getting dusty.

I am not complaining as I have chosen to make climbing, biking and being social essentials. I've put other things on the back burner. It hit me how quickly time flies by, despite what it is you are going through. I want chemo to be over, but I want to take a day before it ends to sit at home and be lazy. I want to take a day after my treatment to take advantage of the free massage and acupuncture that they offer at the cancer center. I want to take the time to have a get together at the end to thank everyone for all they have done.

I thought if anything this disease would teach me to slow down; to take a slow walk in the park, to read on my back porch, to spend the time to make a recipe in Cooking Light. Instead, I feel like it has made me race around, struggle to multitask, and squash as much into the weeks that I feel healthy as possible. Maybe the epiphany comes after you survive the six cycles. Maybe I will never slow down. Maybe it is all relative?

Meanwhile, I don't care about the knitting, or the magazines, or the Cooking Light, or movies. Although I would like to watch one episode each of Orange is the New Black and Game of Thrones, just to say I have seen it. But what I want to do is put all my thoughts on paper. I want to write, I want to read, and I want to plant more flowers in my garden. I want to finish the book, Brown Girls Dreaming. I want to add more poems to this sight and I want the hollyhocks, peonies, and poppies to grow behind my snap dragons and petunias in my garden.

WHITE GIRL DREAMING

July 13, 2015

BROWN GIRL DREAMING, is a book that tells the story of a woman's life through verse. It inspired me to try to write in verse and tell my story. So here is a shorter than book- sized attempt at writing like Jacqueline Woodson.

WRITING DOWN MEMORIES

Brown Girl Dreaming is on my shelf
and a book about my life forming in my head
I want to write about Opa and Oma
Munga and Pop Pop too
about Jeanette and Rancho Bernardo
and how the furniture store grew.

I want to write about our history
About the Shoags and the Pinkuses
About leaving Germany and Lithuania
And about World War Two
The pictures of Sora Razel Bailey
And the family that I never knew.

I want to write about Pop Pop
About him snoring on the couch
About gifts from Munga and Margaret Street
And Opa playing Canoga with me
Having to finish the milk in my bowl
Aunt Helaine, mom, and Uncle Lee

I want to write about our brick town home
About Silver Spring, Maryland
About the green turtle that stored our toys
And the little red table where we used to eat
Flatsy dolls, pink bicycles, Pasha, our dog
Michael and Michelle so attentive and sweet

I want to write about swinging
On our porch on Westview Street
About rope courses, skateboarding, and camping in the backyard
And Brooke and me hiding in the big oak tree
Lauren and her curls and breaking the TV
About lighting nail polish remover and letting the flames run free.
I want to write about watching Oprah
About watching General Hospital with Mom in the rain
About shopping at Willowgrove, Old Navy, and Target
At Beachcombers, swimming in the big pool with Laur
Tennis with Dad, Uncle Frank, and Arthur Ashe
And trying to sleep, but hearing Dad snore.

I want to write about the cousins nine
About the lagoon, Loveladies, and the Jersey shore
About Thanksgiving turkey, sweet potatoes with marshmallow, and more
And how it started with a family of four and then twenty
How we walk in the Wissahicken and play in the leaves
And how we are now forty, how can it be.

I want to write about college
About Alli, Heather, Phaedra, and Toni
About living next to Brueggers Bagels, Ben and Jerrys and the liquor store
And skiing at Mad River, Sugarbush, and Stowe
Swimming in Lake George and hiking Mt. Washington
And wondering what to major in and how I should know

I want to write about going to Israel
About being in the army with Emily
About teaching in Africa and moving to Vail
Racing my mountain bike, competing in the bumps
Dating Chris, Jon, Dan, and now Sandor too
And being healthy and active until finding a lump

I want to write about cancer
About how it hurts, but has not taken my life
About the process of being diagnosed
Wondering what will happen and will I survive
Being scared and frightened
But happy for everyday that I am alive

I want to write so I remember
About all the memories and the good people I know
About the experiences I have had and that have yet to come
So I remember the places and the things I have gotten to see
That have made me the person I am
And will continue to make me the person that I will be

THE DAY
BEFORE FOUR

July 19, 2015

I AM FEELING STRESSED like I am in a time trial race to get everything done before I get zapped again! Gotta climb, bike, hike, grocery shop, pay all my bills and see all my friends before I feel crappy. I watched "The Tour" yesterday and think I would fit in well. I look like all the riders: bald, skinny, with huge quads. I would probably win the time trial. I just finished reading a great book called, Brain on Fire. I highly suggest it. It put my stress into perspective. The author went through much more trauma than I have. It made my case look measly and my need to do everything look very selfish.

I have to say that I have been impressed with what I get done under pressure. This week I tore dozens of baby Aspen suckers out of the ground at one of my gardens. I made cookies and pizza with my little friend, Aviva, for her birthday. I climbed and biked in the rain and cleaned my entire house, top to bottom. The rain has kept me in check, as it has interrupted my activities every day at around 2pm, forcing me to give my body a break. However, the weatherman doesn't know that I am not scared of rain, only thunder and lightning, especially the week before chemo.

Prepping for my parents has been fun! I shopped for all the food I thought they might like to eat: rye bread for mom, bananas for dad, O.J. for breakfast and Utz pretzels for a snack. I went to Home Depot and bought bins to organize my shelves so that my dad wouldn't comment about how messy they look and then rearrange them. I also bought purple pansies to put on the back porch for mom to enjoy while reading her book. I got tickets for the New York Philharmonic and texted my parents to bring their rain coats. No dinner reservations yet, as I am not sure how I will feel. I bought a DiGiorno pizza and rented, "Downtown Abbey" Season 5.

I am hoping to take them for a short hike or at least up the Gondola; the wildflowers are going crazy! There are blues, and purples, fireweed, and wild geranium. Colorado is greener than it has ever been. I wish we could send some rain to California. I am also hoping to take my parents to the beautiful houses where I garden and take Aviva out to lunch. I know my mom will eat her up. Lastly, I want a day to sit in the park with them by the river and on my porch with a bottle of wine. Lots to see and do.

For now, I am going to fit in two more activities: reading my friends article in EAT magazine and going to bed! The time trial is almost over. Tomorrow I can relax while I am fed cocktails.

FIRST TWO DAYS WITH MOM AND DAD

July 26, 2015

LET ME START WITH I LOVE YOU Mom and Dad. I am alive after chemo four. It has been a very busy week. Since most everyone who is reading this is family, you will appreciate this entry. If not, you have family so you can relate. Mom and Dad, I will try to be cute without embarrassing you too much.

I have to admit, I was a little bit nervous for my parents to see me without hair. I know they have seen pictures, but it is different in person. I was also nervous for my dad to see the whole situation. My mom was already here for round one, but my dad has yet to see me sick. However, I think because I look healthy, aside from being bald, it hasn't been too much of a shock.

On Sunday, I went for an early morning ride and my folks arrived around 1pm. I was glad to have one healthy day with them. It was great to catch up and show them that I was really doing OK.

I chose sushi for my last dinner before being zapped. Dad had a Philadelphia roll. My parents were troopers. Despite being tired, we stayed up and talked which kept my mind from thinking about having chemo the next day. The rest of the week was a whir. I feel like it flew by with trying to work, exercise a little bit, entertain, and feel sick. I am not good at multi-tasking in general and it is especially hard when you feel nauseous all the time. However, it was well worth it!

The treatment is always fine for the first few bags as they put the benign fluids in first and then the bad stuff comes at the end. This round was a little bit rougher because my white blood cell counts and my protein counts were lower than they should have been. They almost didn't want to treat me. I guess 1.0 is the magic number and I was at .98. They continued on, thank goodness, as messing with the planned attack can really throw things off.

Mom and Dad stayed for the first half and I had a continuous stream of visitors all morning. It was nice, but sometimes hard for me to stay focused while on Benadryl and whatever else was being administered. Sandor came for the second half of the day. My friend, Amy, who had just completed chemo a month ago and then went off to Thailand, showed up with a full head of curly red hair!! Inspiring!!

I took my short walk around the block after chemo with Mom and Dad instead of Sandor this time and even ate a bit of protein for dinner. I slept hard for half the night, but was awake most of the second half and feeling too sick to write.

I am finding this treatment to be a little bit tougher in terms of my ability to handle the side effects. I do not think that they are much worse, I am just more grossed out by them. I am getting these weird reactions where I can't look at liquid and just writing about the treatment makes me ill. Commercials about food and grocery stores make me queasy and even a bath full of water and the rain make me think of the infusions. It is kind of crazy!!!

Maybe it is just this week. I hope. I have so much more to write, but am going to have to make this a two-part journal as I should run to work. I just wanted to put this up so everyone knows I am alive and my parents are safely at home in Philly after a good dose of Vail, Colorado and me. Hopefully, it isn't too humid and they had a good time even if it wasn't the most relaxing of vacations. Love you guys!!

CARROTS AND PARENTS

July 29, 2015

I AM LYING IN THE DOWNSTAIRS BEDROOM at 3am eating because I have to keep food in my mouth at all times or all I can taste are chemicals. I have moved on from a whole bag of grapes to carrot sticks and am not sure what I'm going to eat next. I can't believe I am saying this, but I am sick of eating!

I waited too long to write and now I have so much to catch up on. Last Tuesday, I couldn't do much. It was a try to feel better day. On Wednesday, my mom, dad, Sandor and I took Avivah, the child for whom I babysit, to the top of the gondola for lunch. We hit the perfect weather window. We walked out to the wedding deck where there is a great view of the back bowls. Dad got to use his fancy camera and took lots of photos. Avivah is in every one. She was the star of the "family." My mom got a text from a friend who asked if the little girl was mine. I'd love to keep her, but her parents might be upset, Sandor too. Avivah did request to spend the night at my house just until my mom leaves.

Thursday Mom came to garden with me while Dad caught up on work. I got twice as much done and even learned that some of the plants that I thought were so pretty were actually weeds. My mom learned that Aspens are a pain in the butt to get rid of because they are connected by one root. You just can't yank one out of the ground! I wish! We both left the garden sweaty, tired, and dirty, but in time to go to the free brass quartet concert at the Interfaith Chapel. Vail has one building that might be a synagogue one day, a church the next, and sometimes even a concert hall.

Friday was another Avivah day and I promised her we would go to the lake. Nottingham Lake is a man-made lake that has been here since I moved to Vail. I have never chosen to spend a day at the lake, however, it is amazing how such an uneventful place can turn into Disney World with a kid. Suddenly, the swings become rocket ships and the sandbox becomes a kitchen for making cakes. The little stream that flows along the perimeter of the playground transforms into a magic swamp full of rainbow worms and unicorn fish. The beach that is maybe 20 yards long is a perfect place to eat a peanut butter and peach sandwich and a plum.

That night I had tickets to see the New York Philharmonic at our outside amphitheater, Ford Park. I couldn't let my parents escape without showing them that, despite Vail being a small town, it has a lot to offer. I took the risk of buying lawn seats; pavilion seats are expensive and hard to get. Unfortunately, and fortunately, in Colorado the weather can turn with the snap of a finger. That night, it never stopped. It started with a drizzle as Bramwell Tobey introduced Mendelssohn's, " Fingal's Cave Overture." It became a steady stream as the orchestra played Grieg's, "Piano Concerto in A Minor Opus 16" and then turned into a downpour for Elgar's, "Enigma Variations, Opus 36."

I always heckle Sandor about bringing too much and being overly prepared, but this time it was appreciated. We were equipped with lawn chairs, elephant size umbrellas, and trash bags to cover our legs. We left the concert shockingly dry considering the amount of water that poured out of the sky that night. It just goes to show that you can defy nature if you have the proper weapons. It also makes you appreciate a warm shower and bed.

I look back on this entry and am so thankful for having such a loving mom to whom everyone is drawn and a dad who has been my number one fan throughout this battle. With my parent's here, I have the most sparkling clean toilets in all of Vail. I have freshly bleached pillow covers on my sofa and new lights to replace the broken ones that plagued my dad throughout his stay. Thank you. (I did leave out meticulous and overly protective as I thought the other qualities overrode those.) I feel so supported by everyone, especially Sandor, who brings me extra blankets at night and restocks the refrigerator with carrot sticks and grapes on a regular basis. I couldn't be luckier.

I look back at this entry and agree with your comments that I do an ungodly amount of activity in one week, even during a chemo week. Life will be so easy when I'm not feeling sick. I want to celebrate and make it to the beach. I'd like to protect myself in case I offended anyone. So, I'll end this entry as I started the last.

Mom and Dad, I love you, if I haven't made that clear.

DRINKING
COFFEE AGAIN

July 30, 2015

I KNOW that I am feeling better when I can drink coffee again in the morning.

I took Saturday off to play, but still was feeling achy and disgusted by everything in the fridge. Sunday I rode up the mountain with two clients whose goal has been to make it from the base at 8,150 to the top 11,570 for a few summers now and they made it! It was great to guide them on the trails, push them to continue, and toast with them over apples and cranberry juice at the summit. I did offer to get Champagne, but they wanted to be able to ride down the single track without breaking any bones!

Sandor called just as I got to the bottom of the mountain to tell me to rush home. Our friend, Page, invited him to the last Bramwell Stovey, New York Philharmonic and had fifth row seats in the pavilion. She told him to bring me! How sweet! Sandor even had a picnic packed. There was salami and Cheez-Its on the counter so I could proteinize before going. Am I spoiled, or what! Ironically, it was sunny and beautiful. Sorry Mom and Dad. I would have given those tickets to you.

Monday, I took a group of young boys up the gondola and down the single track that just opened for the summer due to the heavy rains that we have had. It was fun, but my boys' groups are always so competitive. They yell at each other to keep up, don't wait, and then give the last person a hard time. It is exhausting and makes me nervous! In the afternoon I took the girls up. I know girls are competitive too, just secretly, which is almost worse. However, they always seem to be so much more pleasant to ride with and I am less frightened that they will get hurt. The girls waited for each other, checked in to see if everyone was OK, and even stopped to eat Takis and dance to "Gangum Style."

That night dinner still did not taste good even though Sandor made a huge roast and I made Kasha to go with it so I could get my protein and grains. I ate it, since I know my counts are low, but everything still tasted like chemicals. Likewise, on Tuesday while gardening, the same unpleasant taste remained throughout the day.

However, the acid reflux and gurgling in my stomach began to dissipate. Each hour I seemed to feel a little bit better. After pulling Aspens all day and then power climbing Homestake for two hours with my friend Chris, I went to a bike reunion and gorged myself on pizza and actually could taste it!

It was a great night. I picked up one of my oldest friends, Toni, who grew up in Philly. She was my roommate in college and now lives here in Vail with me. She is uber pregnant! We compared notes nauseous/check, bloated/ check, peeing all the time/check, something kicking you/not check. Darn! Lots in common, minus the result.

We arrived at Pazzos where Tim Young the owner of Vail Bicycle Service where I worked in 1996, had organized a reunion since he was back in town for the week. There, in one room, was everyone I had loved my first year out here and not seen forever. All of us a bit older, wiser, and maybe a little bit more tired, but very much who we were in 1996. Tim's wife, Kathy, looked like she got younger! How does that happen? The only person who looked a century older was their son, Roger, who was a baby when they owned the shop and was now 13. We remember him as the bike shop baby along with Spoke, their dog, and Wheelie, their cat. Funny how one person's memories are not always shared by the person who is remembered.

A blast from the past makes you smile and realize that even though we all have different experiences; we all live the cycle of life. Unfortunately and fortunately, we all get older and gain new memories and older ones become foggy. We all talk about the good old days, back when we were young and had no responsibilities. We all reminisce and joke about how we used to do this and that and couldn't imagine doing that now! It is just "the this and the that" that are different for each person.

Hopefully for me, a part of "the this and the that" will be that I remember how awful everything tasted during chemo, but how I could still eat pizza with my friends and take people biking and climbing. Cancer will just be a part of my story. And today, my coffee tastes really good!

STILL HANGING WITH THE BOYS

August 3, 2015

I HAD A FABULOUS DAY riding Monarch Crest with the boys. I was tentative about going on our traditional Monarch Crest ride as it is long and the boys are fast! However, it is a tradition, and one of my favorite rides in Colorado due to the views, the terrain, and the Chai tea at the Mini Thai Cafe in Poncho Springs. Despite my hesitation, I packed up my backpack with my bike clothes, PB&J and Gorp, and stocked my camelback with water. Then I drank almost a full gallon of water before skipping "Jon Stewart" to go to bed early. In the past, I have always worked through my weekends during the summers. Being sick, I have decided that if I feel good, I don't want to miss out on hanging with my friends before my next treatment.

Bill picked me up at 6:30am. Monarch is about a two -hour drive south to the center of Colorado and the heart of the San Isabel National Forrest. We like to start early because the trail is about 35 miles of winding single track with a 3000ft elevation gain. It begins at 8000 ft. at the base of the original Monarch Crest ski area and tops out at 1100 ft. with a view of Chieti Peak and the Arkansas River. It is just above tree line and high enough that you want to be down in the afternoon before there is any chance of a storm. NOAA called for cloud coverage and a 40% chance of rain in the late afternoon which usually means get off the top of the mountains by 2pm or 3pm because you don't want to get struck by lightning!

It was fun to catch up with Bill on the way to Leadville where we met Jay and John and followed them to Buena Vista for gas and then to the lot where we would park in Poncho Springs. I find it is always hard to wake up early, but then once you get going you forget that the sun has just come up and you could have slept for another two hours. Coffee and good company help too! At the lot, we piled all our stuff into Jay's truck. It is a shuttle ride to Monarch Crest unless you are feeling hardy and want to ride your bike 19 miles up the pass before getting on the single track. I was glad that this option did not come up. I'm sure Bill would have jumped at the opportunity.

The ride starts about 20 miles west of Poncho Springs by the original gondola for the Monarch ski area built in 1939. In the winter, it is no longer used. Tourists line up in the summer to take it to the top so that they can look out over the Southern Rockies. The gondola is an old, rickety shack and I always wonder how it transports and returns the tourists safely. Next to it, is a large modern building with a gift shop, a bathroom, Cliff bars and Gu for the many riders that come to experience this classic trail.

We saddled up: lube, air, helmets, packs! It was predictably windy this early in the morning, but the sky was blue. The trail starts off steep and I knew the boys were going to take off strong. They would want to beat the 20 other riders heading up the road to the single track so we could have it to

ourselves. I was prepared. I bumped my bike into its middle ring, drank a sip of Gatorade, and ground up the dirt, determined to hang.

We hit the single track just before the crew behind us piled up by the sign at the entrance taking over the entire intersection. I unlocked my rear suspension and cranked through the undulating foot width track, swerving through Pinion Pines and Aspens that still held their green leaves. Determined to keep the boys in sight, I bumped it up a gear and pedaled hard feeling the wind try to push me backwards, but failing. The single track drops you onto a pebbly road that grinds uphill to a lookout. A quick snap shot and another single track rolls you south along a ridgeline before hitting a steep ascent to the first peak.

I always like this section, but wonder if I will make it up the climb. John describes it as riding through kitty litter, loose and dirty. After completing it and making it, we gathered at the top to check in for a much needed shake your hands out and take a sip of water break. I enjoy the push of keeping up with Bill, who at 40 something (I won't give it away Bill) always sets high standards for the crew. But, I also know that it is not worth my getting hurt trying to keep up. I was thankful that everyone understood and was willing to take breathers and check in with me every once in a while.

Aside from my back being a little bit sore and my right hand going a bit numb, I was feeling good. The docs said that the nerves in my back might still be recovering from being pinched and that my extremities might be numb. Jay even told me to go ahead on the uphill, saying I was riding fast.

I stayed on John's tail on the downhills which is pretty good considering he has a freeride bike and is an amazing descender. Bill, I never really saw until he stopped at the next section to check in. The fact that he didn't seem agitated by waiting for too long made me think we were all doing OK.

The trail continues to roll into a marshy area past a cabin and then down a road on which you can go thirty miles an hour as long as you are prepared for the hairpin turn at the bottom. It always makes me wonder how Cancellara and Froome make those corners in the Tour without knowing that they are there! The road drops you out by an outhouse where the trail intersects with Starvation Creek, another trailhead. It then continues to climb, turning into windy switchbacks and culminating in a short, but steep, road to the final summit before the descent down Silver Creek to The Rainbow Trail. Thankfully, everyone agreed to a short snack and picture break at our usual spot.

I know it must sound awful to say that we wanted to pass all the other riders at the start. However, it is so much nicer to ride the trail without feeling you are going to be run over or that you are going to run over someone else. It has been a tradition for us to ride this together every year. It is a treat to have a crew that keeps a similar pace and has similar abilities. A four to five -hour ride can turn into an eight -hour nightmare if you don't have the skills to ride it. This has been the case on many of my past Monarch trips and it is a relief to be with four people who know the trail and what it entails.

The lookout point is always a great spot to eat. You know you have a long decent along Silver Creek before hitting the Rainbow Trail that takes you back into Poncho Springs. Jay breaks open his turkey sandwich and John his Coke and Lays Potato Chips, while Bill munches on a Cliff Bar. Jay is the biggest and the quietest of the crew. I always wonder how he can blow us away on the climbs as he is built to descend. John is tall, but skinny and ironically climbs slower than Jay, but he rocks on the descents. Bill is the enduro man. He puts in more miles a week than I put in all summer and he eats like a rabbit. I just pray and seem to do alright.

The drop into Silver Creek is fast and smooth before becoming very rocky and technical. It then crosses a two-plank bridge and continues along the creek to a rooty uphill. There it connects with the Rainbow intersection and an opt-out on a dirt road that connects to highway 50 back into Poncho Springs. The Rainbow Trail is my favorite part as it winds up and down and across creeks and meadows towards the last campground ascent to the final downhill. Like the rest of the ride you must pay attention as every creek crossing is followed by a steep kitty litter uphill that will make your wheels spin out and push your cardiovascular abilities to their fullest. I kept telling myself, leave space and weight the back wheel or be prepared to walk.

The end of the Rainbow Trail is always tricky because you are tired and think you are done just as you hit another creek crossing. Luckily we were all on the same page and rode cautiously to the rocky switchbacks where the trail hits the road. Smiling and ready for the smooth asphalt neck into Poncho Springs for lunch. We high-fived just as it began to drizzle. I took a breath, relieved that I had hung for the entire ride. I know the trail well and would not have gotten lost or hurt, but was secretly overjoyed to be able to still keep up with the boys.

Even though I have set my goals to be different this year, healing, having fun, and trying not to get hurt, it is rewarding to be able to do the activities I would normally do, considering my situation. It surprises me that I am able to stay fit, with little or no pain, on the weeks that are not chemo weeks. I think of all the people I know who have or have had cancer and hope that they are able to carry on with some of their regular routines and traditions while going through treatment as I find it is so important for healing.

GONE FISHING

August 4, 2015

TODAY, SANDOR MADE ME GO FISHING. Doctor's orders were to chill out and not be active before my pet scan tomorrow. Sandor knows that sitting still is not my forte so he stuck me on a boat and got us lost in his brother's marina. As much as I would never choose to spend the day fishing, I appreciated the gesture. In the end, I found it quite relaxing until the reservoir turned into an ocean.

We drove over on Monday after my ride with the boys. Sandor has had these visions of setting up a climbing area for his brother's fishing clients. I love the theory, but am not sure by looking at the people who choose to fish, that rock climbing would be at the top of their list of activities. Regardless, I felt like after all of his support, the least I could do is help him bolt some routes. Besides, his crazy ideas always seem to become lucrative in the long run.

So, we spent Monday playing Lewis and Clark and exploring rocks and jumping fences to see what was BLM land and what was 11-mile marina land. Sandor carried the drill and I carried the ropes. We found two rocks that we deemed worthy for setting up routes. They were long enough to be challenging, but not so long that they would scare off a beginner or so we thought. We climbed through a skinny canyon between two rocks and shuffled up the backside to set an anchor. When we got to the top, we realized that we had brought all the essential bolting materials, but had forgotten the anchors!

We spent a while creating a make shift anchor out of a rock at the top of the climb using an old rope and some locking beamers. It was a good thing we did a trial climb as the moss-covered limestone proved to be slippery and lacked any features to hold onto. We tried climbing the left side of the rock, then the right and decided to drill some holes since we had rented a drill. We left the holes to be filed with anchors the next time we returned. We had to make the drive and the renting of the drill worthwhile since we forgot the most essential part.

Sandor and I went back to his brother's cabin and ate lunch with him. Then we went back and explored and drilled more anchor holes until shadows crept over the reservoir and the sun began to sink behind the Mosquito Range. The views were beautiful and I was spent and feeling more OK with the idea of being stuck fishing all day on Tuesday.

After steaks and french fries and a good night sleep, we woke up at the crack of dawn to prepare the boat and the lures for the day. Sandor convinced me to buy a fishing license again. I used last year's license all of two times. I bought a fishing report so I could know where to "troll" for the day even though I didn't know what that meant. I was hoping I would have beginners luck and Larry would be patient with my lack of ability to pay attention to his directions while playing tug of war with a trout.

We set out onto the shimmering water. I did get the first bite, but I also lost the first bite. Dang this multi- tasking thing. Fish two came to Sandor with ease, but was too small to keep. Then I caught a big one, but it snapped the line. Guess I am not beginner enough to have beginner's luck. I was starting to give up hope and feeling a bit claustrophobic when Sandor caught a good one worthy of keeping. We would have dinner for the night!

As the fish swam around in the tank and Sandor and Larry quoted Kenny and Cartman from South Park, the waves grew bigger and I had to hold my hat on my head. We turned the boat around as the trees and the tents along the shore billowed in the wind. Larry sped up the boat and you could hear it crash as we bumped against the white capped water, sending it splashing over the rain shield and past our heads. Sandor and Larry ducked and grumbled as I squealed with laughter as a bucket worth of water splashed up against Sandor's back and soaked his sweatshirt and hair.

So much for a relaxing boat ride! However, it did keep me from biking and climbing, gave me a good laugh, and left us with fish for dinner. We had the dock boys filet the trout and then snuck some Mud Pie ice cream bars from the freezer. We gave Larry a big thank you and headed off to Fairplay, over Hoosier Pass and back to Vail. We returned the drill and sat in traffic through the construction zone at Dowd Junction. Psyched to be home, on land, and have fresh trout, we opened the cooler to find we had left it at Larry's.

I'm starting to wonder if chemo brain is catchy as Sandor never forgets anything. Oh well. I guess the trip served its purpose. It made me chill and pizza was a good back up dinner. However, I am not sure fishing will be my future sport!

99% CANCER FREE

August 7, 2015

YEAH!! I AM ALMOST CANCER FREE. The scan showed one little dot and a bunch of inactive cells hanging out in my abdomen. My heart lit up. My kidneys lit up, and the rest of me looked like it did before I got diagnosed with Lymphoma! That is good! Hopefully, the one little dot that still has metabolic activity will go away after my last two chemo sessions.

It was a long day as I hate not playing, not working, and wasting the whole day at the hospital. As Sandor put it, "Your life is more important than $120 or a ride up the mountain!" I agree, but I was still planning on finding a way to squish in all three. I had to be at Shaw at 8am, then again at 1:20, and then at the dentist at 4pm. I could do a short ride from 11-1, then eat ice cream and respond to my emails before 4, and fit in one more short ride before going home to make dinner. We'll see how it goes.

I had a tech who was super sweet. She had blond hair and looked to be in her late twenties. She started with   putting the dye into my IV and telling me to sit still so it could distribute throughout my body. No texting, no reading; she didn't want the scan to pick up any extraneous activity. So I sat, once again, for 45 minutes letting the tracer flow through me. I could talk so I asked the tech if she liked being in medicine. She said she would rather be a nurse. She didn't like nuclear medicine because you send the patients into the PET scan and, if they test positive, you never see them again. She also told me how they did shifts working with nuclear medicine so they wouldn't be in danger and that the door was sealed to keep her safe and she would leave while I absorbed the chemicals. I don't think she was sensitive enough to calm a patient waiting for a pre-scan of her future.

After mentioning that the scanner was being temperamental, she told me to be still and call her if I needed anything. I prepared myself for the half hour of photos; taking off my jewelry and wiggling and scratching everything that might itch while under the machine. Despite my preparation, within the first slide, I was already thinking about the itch that was forming on my left shoulder. Then it was my cold toes and my fingers; they were numb. I closed my eyes and thought about the beach. It worked for a minute and then my thoughts came back to what will the scans show. Then to, did Tom murder Megan in The Girl on the Train or was it her husband Scott? I wondered if I could fit in a short ride between the scan and meeting with Dr. Alec? I felt pretty ADD and tried to come back to my beach scene and hold it in my brain for the second part of the scan: sun, waves, warmth!

I got dressed quickly and rushed off to deliver my oatmeal raisin cookies to some friends who have cancer and are sick. I had to do it today before Sandor eats them. I decided I could fit in two more appointments and a quick ride. I rushed up the mountain and rode a single track in the wrong direction. I was thinking this is how it goes when you have a family and only

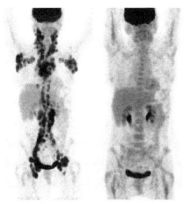

Baseline study   After chemotherapy

an hour to exercise. You have to go fast and be efficient, so I did exactly that and made it back to pick up Sandor for my 1:20.

I know Sandor thinks I squish way too much into my day, so I did not bring up the ride, just the errands. I thought if I fit in my activities and was on time, it would all be good. Of course, all was going according to plan until I couldn't find my keys. Essential things! I finally gave up, got my spare key and rushed back to Shaw. Sandor was shaking his head the whole way. Typical me.

Dr. Alec wasn't mad and he sat us down, pulled up my scan from April, and then from today. The changes were huge. As I said, the majority of the indolent cells in my stomach were gone and all of the high-grade cells in my butt, groin, chest, and lungs had disappeared. It was cool to compare the two slides. They looked like, what I imagine, a skeleton would look like if you were on acid; fluorescent rainbow colored and swirly with polka dots. But the second scan had no polka dots and my heart which was not lit up in the first scan was now lit up. In the first scan, the cancer was using up all the sugar, but now there was nothing to steal it away from my heart.

We topped the day off with a chocolate milk shake from Marble Slab. Perfect thing before my dentist appointment! Apparently, the chemo has affected my mouth and things keep falling out. This time it was the chip that they fixed on my front tooth, leaving me looking like a bald farmer with a hole in my mouth. I wasn't too concerned about the look as I have learned that anything goes. I was concerned about the nerves and the possibility of not being able to eat ice cream after having chemo. It was an easy hundred dollar fix. I should have been a dentist or a plumber! It looks much better and I have no food limitations. So, worth the money. And obsessive me, still fit in a short ride after getting my tooth fixed, which once again, I didn't mention to Sandor. Shhhhh!! Good thing he doesn't read my blog! Knock on wood!

I WAS NEUTROPENIC!!

August 10, 2015

I WAS NEUTROPENIC! I didn't even know what that meant two months ago! It is crazy how you can feel so great and not even know you are sick. I worked all day Saturday and climbed all day Sunday and even stayed awake for the Ballantine Ballet. It was beautiful, but slow. I did get to see Misty Copland though and it kept my mind busy so I wouldn't think about being chemotized. I woke up ready and prepared to tackle one more round and here I am googling how to increase my white blood cell count.

I made the mistake of eating like a pig thinking last night was my last night for everything to taste good for a while. I had two helpings of pumpkin lasagna, peanut butter chocolate chip cookies, and I even had a glass of wine. I took my Prednisone and put my EMLA cream on my port to numb it so it could be accessed by the nurses. I packed my book and my computer (that I never end up using) and had my final cup of coffee for the week. Got into Sandor's car prepared for battle.

Forty-five minutes and 22 cubic centimeters of blood later, I went to meet with Dr. Alec. He was friendly and calm as always. We chatted about Sandor having a new phone and the complications of having big fingers and trying to text. We discussed his kids enjoying their summer and I asked him about taking Ibuprofen before chemo to help with the headache chemo gives me. He said nothing, just smiled, then said, "Yes, but not today because you are not having chemo."

I thought it was a joke and said, "Cool, Guess I am better!" He smiled back and said, " No, seriously." I felt just fine so I thought maybe they decided my scans were so I good I didn't need any more treatment. He turned the computer towards me and pointed to my WBC (white blood count) and the .60 next to it. Last week I was .98 which is low, as the magic number is 1.0, but .60 means definitely, NO CHEMO. If your counts are that low and then they drop even more from the chemotherapy, you will be at high risk for infection and not be able to fight it. In my case, although most of the cells are gone, the risk does not outweigh the benefits.

It was a bit stressful to get all prepared and be rejected. It was frustrating to have to re-arrange work yet again. BUT, it sure is nice to have another few days to feel good. This is the longest break I have had yet between treatments. It is going to be a real tease to go in again on Thursday and get knocked down if my counts are better.

I have not found any studies that have real proof of ways to get my WBC up. Alec reminded me several times that this happens and just like cancer it is nothing I did and there is nothing I can do to improve my counts except get a shot of Neulasta. The side effects are possible spleen rupture and Sickle Cell Crisis, lung problems and bone pain. I guess I should get over worrying

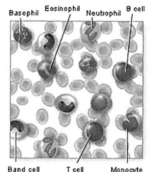

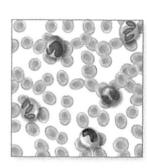

Basophil Eosinophil Neutrophil B cell

Band cell   T cell   Monocyte

about side effects considering what I am going through, but they still make me a little bit nervous.

Studies say eat protein, take zinc, eat garlic and yogurt. They say wash your hands all the time and stay away from sick people. They say exercise releases the cells that are holding onto the marrow and shift them into your blood stream. I don't have yogurt at home, so I had chocolate ice cream. I had a pork tenderloin for dinner and put some garlic salt on my macaroni and cheese. It didn't taste very good. I am staying away from crowds and I have the cleanest hands in the world. Exercise, well that's an easy one!

Wish me luck on Thursday. As much as I would love to put off chemo, I know that it is better to plug away and get it over with!

PARANOIA

August 13, 2015

I SPENT THE LAST TWO DAYS being PARANOID: paranoid about germs, paranoid about exercising too much, paranoid about eating properly. I read every article I could find on how to increase your white blood cells. There wasn't much information, but there was a lot of information on how dangerous it is for them to be low. The few pieces of advice that I found helpful were moderate your exercise and eat garlic and protein. To stay healthy, an article suggested staying away from crowded places, washing your hands a lot, and not going near anyone who is sick.

These are not hard tasks, except for this week, when I had so much planned. On Tuesday, I planned to garden all day, go for a ride, and then to girls' night out. Instead, I gardened half a day, I bailed on the ride, and made spaghetti with garlic for dinner, and went out with the girls, but left when they went to the crowded bar.

On Wednesday, I had planned to babysit in the morning, bike with a family in the afternoon, and then go on a ride before seeing Martha Cohn speak about being a Jewish spy during WWII. I babysat half a day, cut the family ride in half and skipped going on my own ride. I did go to the speaker, but avoided hugging anyone.

I went in today thinking that there was no possible way that I could have increased my WBC count to 1.0 or above if it was .6 on Monday. I was feeling tired and run down, possibly from cancer, and possibly from doing too much. I had a cold and my temperature was higher than normal. I let them draw my blood and was sure that they would send me home, but as it turned out, I was at 1.4 that is .4 above what I needed to be.

I am not sure how this all works and I am not sure that the doctors are either. There are too many variables to know why my counts went up because I exercised less, ate protein, didn't go to the bars, or just got lucky. I could have done the opposite and had my counts be too low. I am beginning to think that this is just how cancer goes. It is a game that you have minimal control over.

It was a long chemo session. For some reason, I was more disgusted and nauseous than I have been in the past. They say the last two treatments are hard because the effects are cumulative. It definitely feels that way. But I have five down now and only have one more to go!!!

DONE

August 16, 2015

COMMENTS

Jenny, the Conqueror. Keep it going. One more to go.
 —Teresa, August 17, 2015

Jenny,
You put us into the feelings, tastes and emotions quite well. It helps us understand a little better what you are going through. Only going through the same situation would give us a full understanding, but you are doing a great descriptive job. Thank you for your great writing brave lady.
 —Uncle Lee and Aunt Barbara,
  August 16, 2015

I love your poem! It is so evocative and wonderfully understated. (And this praise comes from a poetry major, so don't discount it!)
 —Linda, August 16, 2015

A SIDE NOTE that I am functioning and worked the last two days, but this is how I am feeling right now.

DONE

I am done with feeling hungover when I didn't even drink
I am done with the headaches and the dizziness
I am done with the aches the chills and the hot flashes
Done with the fatigue the queasiness and the pain

I am done with the taste of Oncovin and Adriamycin
I am done with nightmares and waking up in the middle of the night
I am done with eating all of the time when I am not hungry
Done with the chemo and feeling sick

I am done with feeling faint when I hear words associated with cancer
I am done with thinking about how to fit everything in and be sick
I am done with making medical and financial decisions
Done with feeling guilty for taking time to do what I want when I feel well

RAIN

Crack bam boom
The crash of the thunder
Silences I-70
There are no cars
Only the rush of the rain
Hitting the skylight
In heavy pellets

It is like early summer
When the snow melts
And the Gore Creek runs high enough
To block the sound
Of the semis that rumble
Towards their destinations

For a moment
I forget about the nausea
The throbbing in my head
The taste of my lips
I forget about my thirst
My aches and my chills
And listen to the rain

Then I curl up in a ball again
And try to sleep

MOM'S ALWAYS RIGHT

August 17, 2015

MOM IS ALWAYS RIGHT
Even at forty
She keeps giving me books of verse
I think she knows me best

And now here I am
Trying to write in verse

Not thinking about being sick
But thinking about Mira
And her dad who is dying from Aids
And how I want to write like she does

How at such a young age
She is so much more eloquent
Than I ever will be
But I will try

Parched
My throat swollen
It is one a.m.

I sip some Limeade blhhhh

I start where I left off
Mira's dad is gay
He has cheated on mom

Maybe Pepsi will taste better blhhhhhh

Mira's senior year is not going well
She's lost interest in school
She's lost her yearbook job
Now dad has AIDS

We could fix that now
Maybe we'll be able to fix lymphoma then

I come up with Limeade mixed with seltzer
Better
Boom Chica Popcorn
Comes with it

Mira shuts everyone out
Studies the stars

84

Gets rid of her boyfriend
Decides who is really important
Interviews her dad
Hugs him before he dies

I cry
I am not thinking about feeling nauseous
I am thinking life is short
Too short to be silent
To wait to do what you want

I am thinking about trying to write
Like the author
Cordelia Jenson
Who I think is Mira
But I do not know yet

I am thinking I should fly home
For the lymphoma walk
And that I am lucky to have
Such a supportive family

I am thinking that some people
Would not like this book
But I do

And there will be a cure for me
Like there is for AIDS

The sky is still full of stars
There is no reason
To think that
There is no hope

I am thinking
Mom is always right
I will read more verse

THE THINGS I CANNOT STAND

August 17, 2015

THE THINGS I CANNOT STAND

I cannot stand
Cranberry juice
The smell of soap
Jolly Ranchers
They remind me
Of the popsicles
I am given
During chemo

I can't stand
Hearing the word Adriamycin
Or writing it
Seeing the Cancer Center
Or reading the pamphlets
Glowing with fake bald smiles
Telling me which drugs to take
And why

I can't stand looking at myself
When I Facetime my family
Seeing my eye lashes
That have turned to
A whisper
And stare at me
With unneeded pity

One more day
And two weeks
Hopefully all those things
That I cannot stand will
Go away

COMMENTS

Hi Jenny,
Two poems! Distilled with the essence of your thoughts and feelings, transforming the difficulties of your illness/treatment experience into art...so important for you and touching others. Glad you're finding some pleasure being in the sun... hope the ordinary pleasures of food will be coming back soon. Love and healing thoughts :-)
   —Ruth and Barry, August 17 2015

MY PROVIDER AND PESSIMIST

The sun fills the sky
I have the day for
Us to be together
No gardening
No babysitting
No guiding
Just us

I suggest a climb
Wherever he wants to go
But there is an upstream trough
And a combination of jet maxima aloft

I think in my head
We will be fine

So let's bike
By our house
Where the world
Is still yellow
And there are no
Cumulous clouds
To form moisture in the air

It is too hot
How do people live
In 87% temperatures?
It is perfect I think
A hike Booth Falls
We can sit
By the broken Choke Cherry
On the granite ledge
Where the wind
From the water fall
Sends chills up your spine

Not today
I hiked yesterday

I shift not knowing
Whether to run
Or let the guilt
Of wanting to play on the

First and only day
I will have off in two weeks
Permeate

Whether I should
Succumb to coffee
That I cannot taste
Cereal that makes me ill
And reading the paper
Which we do everyday
Or go soak in some Vitamin D

I smile
Put on my hat
And leave
Not sure what I
Will do
Next

MORE POEMS

August 21, 2015

105

He is 65 I am 41
He sings Ramble on Rose
I sing Time After Time
He quotes Abbott and Costello
And I quote Bill Cosby
He remembers 19 cent McDonalds burgers
I remember when they were a dollar
His first car was an MGD
Mine was an Acura Integra
His photos black and white
Dad fighting World War II
Mine colored
Mom and dad in bell bottoms
He chooses house chores and buys me flowers
I work, climb, bike and make him cookies
Dinner is nice then Colbert then Stewart
Parties are fun, I prefer to read or write
Together we sing Southern Cross
Dance to the Dirty Dozen Brass Band
And laugh at re-runs of South Park
Together we eat ten dollar burgers in Vail
Drive our Subarus' off road
And share iPhone photos
Of climbing, skiing, and biking through the woods
Together, he makes sure I take my Prednisone
And I make sure he takes his pills
Together we go to Sushi
And with friends to The Samples Concert in the Park
He falls asleep with the TV on
Me with a journal and a book by my head
He is 65 and I am 41
Together we are 105 but really ageless
Most of the time

FIRES IN CALIFORNIA

The dust kicks up
The sky thick with smoke
The trail meanders North
But I cannot see the skyline
I know this bike ride well
But it is different today
Hard to breathe
Because of the chemo
Because of the thick air
There are no clouds
The sky is grey not blue
There is a smell of a campfire
That has been put out
I picture fields ablaze
Trees piles of red embers
My one little cell
That still burns orange
The chemicals that are attacking my body
The men that are fighting the flames
I ride harder
Into the smoke

ACUPUNCTURE

August 22, 2015

YESTERDAY, I HAD ACUPUNCTURE. I was seven days out of my fifth chemo. The cancer center gives you six free treatments of acupuncture or massage. I only used one, so thought I should try acupuncture. I've had dry needling in the past for a sports injury and didn't like having pins stuck into me. However, everyone told me acupuncture is amazing and eases many of the side effects of chemo. After canceling three of my appointments, I was determined to make this one.

The caveat to the free treatment is that it must be on Thursday and they are only available until three. This makes it hard if you are working full time. My chemo treatment changed to the day I had planned for acupuncture. I barely made it due to a late start for a hike to Lost Lake with some clients. I was sure Eliza was going to ban me from my free procedures if I missed this one. So, I made my clients hike, eat quickly, and drove fast down the bumpy Red Sandstone dirt road. I told them it was part of the adventure. I hope they hike with me again in the future.

Eliza, the acupuncturist, is a curly blond haired mother of two. She has a soft voice and perfect skin and was dressed in a blue wraparound dress that matched her eyes. She walked me into a room with dimmed lights, two lounge chairs, and a table. I liked her right away, but was still weary of having needles stuck in me. She asked about my diagnosis and about my treatment and future prognosis. She jotted down some notes so that I was in her computer system and asked me what symptoms were bothering me the most.

After telling her about my constant headache, feeling nauseous, everything tasting terrible, and my hot and cold flashes, she told me that she would put needles in the points along my body that relieve stress and help with digestion. She told me that acupuncture originated in China in 100B.C. She explained that there is a chart with meridians that show different acupuncture points. She would trigger specific points with tiny needles and then leave me in the room to relax for twenty minutes and let the needles work their magic and ease my pain. I liked the idea of easing the pain, but not the idea of the needles. Heck though, after all I have been through, what did I have to lose.

She had me lie on the table and sensing my nerves about the needles, turned on some background nature music and told me to relax. She said they were tiny needles and I would barely feel them. If one of the needles hurt, she would just take it out. I shut my eyes and pretended the waves crashing in the background were real and that I was really lying on the beach. It worked. I barely felt them. One or two gave me a slight prick, but that was about it. I lay there scared to move as she dimmed the lights even more and left me lying on the table reminding me to relax. I found this hard to do and felt more like a beached porcupine.

Twenty minutes seemed like an eternity. I wanted to peek at the needles, but I was scared to see them and to, nervous to move. I thought about a Saturday Night Live episode where the acupuncturist kept hitting the wrong points and blood kept flying out from everywhere. Every twitch made me think that I was going to have a muscle spasm and I had an itch on my ear where she had placed two needles in a row. I planned the rest of my day, re-worked my different vacation ideas, and calculated my last week's earnings. Anything not to think about the needles.

Finally, the time was up. Eliza asked me how I felt. I wasn't sure if I was supposed to feel instant satisfaction or wait a day or two to feel the results. Relieved, I answered that I was ready for the needles to be pulled out. I have read many research articles on acupuncture and there seem to be varied opinions about its effectiveness. Some say that it relieves specific muscle pains, but others say that the symptoms are cured purely due to the placebo effect. I figure either way, if it makes me feel less ill, it doesn't matter what causes the reaction.

I am one day out of acupuncture and the results are still unclear. I wish that I had had treatment on a day immediately after chemo when I was really feeling ill. I have eaten a little more today and was able to go to the bathroom, something that has been a continuing challenge the week after treatment, so those are pluses. I am not sure that I am more relaxed, but I did not see my intensity and insane amount of energy to be an issue. I don't know that relaxed for me would be visible. It just might make me normal. I did like the ocean music though and will either do a massage or one more acupuncture after my final treatment.

GOT MY BUTT KICKED

August 24, 2015

LAST TIME I HUNG WITH THE BOYS, I did fine. This time I got my butt kicked. I feel like the effects of chemo have no real schedule. Usually, by a week out, the side effects are starting to go away and my energy level is getting back to normal. This time the side effects did decrease, but my energy level has just not come back. I am sure it didn't help that I worked the last ten days in a row before riding with the boys, but I just can't seem to get my mojo.

I was looking forward to riding the Colorado Trail all week. I bought Cliff bars, made a PB&J, and stuffed suckers and a bag of GORP in my pack. I drank tons of water, which has been a challenge for me, and got up early to drive over the pass to Copper. I cruised past the roundabouts filled with magenta and yellow snap dragons and bright orange marigolds. They had doubled in size since the start of the summer. I wondered if they liked being fed steroids.

John was waiting at the ski parking structure that was free in the summer. The other boys had bailed, so at least I only had to keep up with one person! We biked over to the bottom of Copper ski area. A dirty white half pipe rose out of the lush green base and a group of kids in snowboard gear were hiking along its side. Copper is known for Woodward, a training gym for the U.S. Freestyle team. They leave their Freestyle Park open as long as possible. I didn't realize that meant August!

Janet's Cabin to Searle Pass is one of my favorite summer rides. We usually add Kokomo Pass and drop into Camp Hale on the other side of the mountain range. The ride starts at the west end of Copper Mountain and follows Guller Creek 8 miles up a windy, single track to Janet's Cabin. It starts at 9,758 ft. and reaches the cabin at 11,610 ft. and the start of Searle Pass at 12,027. At the top, you are above tree line and the air is thin.

John rode off on his 27.5 Santa Cruz. This means he has the new, bigger wheels and is ahead of me more than he usually is. I am used to being able to push a bit harder and keep everyone in sight, but today I was huffing from the start. The fireweed danced in the wind while showy daisies welcomed me up the trail. We rode through Aspens and Pines, over roots and rocks. I like to keep going, afraid I will quit if I stop to rest. But, today it was necessary.

John was patient and listened to me whine that I couldn't keep up and was tired. He smiled and said not to be too hard on myself. We sat in the shade and took pictures of the flowers, drank some Gatorade and plugged on. Indian Paintbrush and larkspur dotted the fields ahead and the trail grew rockier. The colors were vivid: bright, yellow goldenrod and deep, blue harebells. At the top, the flowers disappeared and the sky opened to a view of Mt. Democrat and Mt Lincoln to the South and the Gore Range to the North.

Exhausted, we hid behind a rock to shelter us from the wind. We drank bing cherry juice and ate gorp and peanut butter sandwiches. I was happy to be at the top, but disappointed at my lack of energy. You could hear goats in the distance, but otherwise it was silent. No I70, no TV, no nurses, just us and the wind. The trip down was fast and beautiful. It took half the time it took to ascend, but resulted in double the injuries. I couldn't seem to stay on my bike. I fell on a root crossing a creek and again riding over a skinny wooden bridge. I tumbled down the trail and hugged a few trees. This was not like me, as my strength is usually the descents.

I finally arrived where the Colorado Trail met the Copper mountain ski run, beat up and frustrated. Usually, on John's tail, he was surprised I had taken so long. It was definitely not a typical Jen performance, but I survived. Maybe the doctors are right that the effects are cumulative. I was happy to change out of my bike clothes and be back where the roundabout flowers were fed drugs. Despite my injuries, I would do it again in a heartbeat. However, I do hope to ride better next weekend!

IGNORANCE
IS BLISS

August 26, 2015

I MADE THE MISTAKE of calling my nurse to ask a few questions today and found out that it is sometimes better not to know than to know. Ignorance is bliss because you can't worry if you don't know what to worry about. I had some burning questions about upcoming plans. I figured I am the risk taker and Sandor leans toward the conservative side. I was hoping Katie would be my middle man, my decision maker. She was wonderful. However, she did not give me the black and white answers I wanted. She told me the best and worst case scenarios and left it up to me to decide. Great! Something I am so good at!

My first question—Can I start substitute teaching as most of my summer jobs are coming to an end? I think I knew the answer, but wanted to hear it from her. She said that she likes patients to be able to go on with their normal lives, but reminds me my white blood cell count is probably lower than it was last time, making my immune system very weak. She said do it if I really want to, but if it is avoidable that would be a safest choice. The risk is probably not worth the reward.

My second question was pretty much answered by the first. I was planning to go to the Black Canyon this weekend with my friend Sarah. This is a canyon where you hike into the lowest point and then climb three, four, eight pitch climbs to get back to the top. We are both good climbers and I am sure the actual rock ascent will be manageable. The problem is that we are 2 hours away from service and medical facilities if I get neutropenic or get hurt. For most people injuries and colds are not so much of a worry, but for me it could mean blood fusions and, worst case scenario, stem cell transplants. All sound fairly unpleasant.

The final question involves my desire to leave here as soon as I complete my treatments and take a Vail vacation. This one had a more positive response. My hope was to go away the last week of September and climb with the girls in Las Vegas. Because of my postponed treatments, I will only be three weeks out of my final chemo. However, I will be close to a city and hopefully recovering by then. Katie seemed to be sure this would work out.

I asked her about coming in to take my blood counts so I would feel better about going away this weekend. She said it is sometimes better to gauge it on how you feel and not on numbers, as they can be deceiving. She said most people feel weak and like they are on the verge of getting sick when their counts are really low. But, if I don't feel that way and don't know my counts, I should just plug on and be aware of the consequences. I asked her if she would go on this trip. She said not even if she was healthy! Then she said it is hard to say, if not in my shoes, but that it is all over soon so why not wait a few more weeks.

Like I said ignorance is bliss, but maybe, in my case, it is better to know.

ADVENTURES IN THE BLACK CANYON PART I

August 31, 2015

WHAT AN ADVENTURE! I called Sarah a half a dozen times this week to question her about our climbing trip to the Black Canyon of the Gunnison. How far is the drive? How hard are the climbs? What is the weather pattern in Gunnison? What if my blood counts are too low? Then I changed my mind a million times. I was going. I wasn't going. I was going. I wasn't going. On Friday around 3 p.m., Sarah picked me up and the decision was made. I would be climbing The Escape Artist, a 5.9 grade III mountain, and camping despite my white blood cells being below .5 and without anyone wishing me a safe trip. I figured, if I got a fever, Aspen was not far and if I died, at least it would be in a beautiful spot.

We arrived late Friday after stopping for food, gas, and a wrong turn in Peonia. The ride was scenic as Highway 133 cruises along the Crystal River and through the almost nonexistent towns of Redstone and Marble. Marble consists of 1st through 4th street and a coal mine. The turn off to 92 takes you through Crawford which has a liquor store. Then the road turns to dirt. You pass by a forest service building and then reach the campground; a circular road spotted with tents that surround a wooden restroom.

As we pulled in a full moon rose behind us and lit up the walls of the canyon. We put up our tents and sat by the edge of the site where the ground ended and dropped into a huge chasm carved by the Gunnison River. Sarah has been working towards her AMGA rock guide course. They require you to lead a certain amount of category three climbs. These are climbs that take a day to complete due to technical difficulty on the approach and can be any level of climbing.

We had downloaded Mountain Project and taken a picture of the Black Canyon Guide book pages. We also copied the write -up for the climb. Our bags were packed with a day's worth of food, rain jackets, and tape. We woke up early, ate eggs, and summer sausage and put on all our gear for the descent into the canyon. We hiked down with another couple from Vail. The gully was steep and full of loose rocks and Poison Ivy. We walked carefully, knowing that a sprained ankle or big fall could be very difficult to deal with on this terrain. As the river got closer and the walls grew bigger, we reached the base of The Escape Artist.

It was intimidating, rated a 5.9, but with a huge traverse making it difficult for both the leader and the follower. It also boasted of a 5.10-pitch just above the traverse known for having many faces, but not having many places for gear. As we stared up at our future pitches, I knew that Sarah was going to be at the limit of her climbing ability and I was not going to be much help if we got into dire circumstances. I am strong but wimpy when it comes to long alpine routes.

We took one last pee break and as I was replacing my harness, I heard a yelp and a cry from the other side of the tree. Sarah who is the calmest most leveled headed and humble person I know, had pulled out her IV that connects to her insulin pump. I could see her frustration as tears welled up in her eyes. She had spent a summer of preparing mentally and physically for this climb, but knew there would be severe repercussions if she attempted it without insulin. A risk not worth the reward! She took a deep breath and we waved and wished Ben and Ariel a good climb and headed silently back up to the campground.

She apologized to me but I was secretly feeling like it was a sign that an easier climb might be a better option. We trudged back up the gully leaving our gear at a shorter easier option called the Casual Off Route. It was still grade III and rated 5.8 with 7 pitches of climbing. Perfect for me! Despite her disappointment I could feel the weight lifted off both of our shoulders knowing this was much more at our level. It was one Sarah had climbed before, making me feel much more relaxed about the day.

We got a super late start after doubling our approach. Luckily, the weather was in the 80's with clear skies. We would be baking on the rock, but would hopefully stay dry. Sarah led the first three pitches as they were rated harder. I am a good sport climber and have been climbing longer than Sarah. However, in the last few years she has surpassed me by far through her dedication to working to improve her trade skills. She has become amazingly strong, a good route finder, and has an uncanny ability to stay calm under pressure. She is smooth, confident, and willing to take risks. Quite the opposite of me.

Sarah's strength is crack climbing and mine is face climbing, making us good partners. I had a lot to work on as far as Alpine climbing goes. We swapped off and on. I led the easier pitches. Sarah was scared with every move I made. She led the harder pitches smiling and yelling about how much she loved cracks. We worked our way up the pink-streaked Pegmatite and the long winding crack systems. By pitch seven, I was more than glad we had not climbed The Escape Artist, finding this to be plenty of a challenge.

We topped out around 6:30 at the trail leading back to the campground. We made our way through the Pinyon and Juniper glad to be on steady ground and escape the blazing heat. We set our gear on the table, relieved to take the weight off our hips, and joined Ariel and Ben back on the edge of the canyon we had just climbed. We shared stories, compared body parts that hurt, and complained about rope drag. Listening, I thought that some higher power was watching over us when Sarah's pump came off. We shared our thoughts about tomorrow agreeing not to attempt anything big. As we made dinner, the moon, once again, made an appearance in the unblemished sky and cast its shadow across the next climb that we would attempt.

ABOVE THE GUNNISON

The river runs green
The foam gathers in white clouds
Bubbling and passing through the rocks
Calm pools of aquamarine rest below
The painted wall rises behind us
Pegmatite stripes like veins across the black granite
Voices echo and respond across the canyon
Off belay, that's me, climb on
Off belay, that's me, climb on
Chirping sparrows twitter in circles
While the raven makes an echoing croak
A lizard sprints across the rock and stares
The day grows hotter we bake in the sun
Sarah slides the nuts against the uneven rock
I carefully pull them out
I place the Camelots, testing their strength
Sarah frees them and climbs on
We twist up the gearless faces
And wedge ourselves into the cool cracks
Jamming knees, hands, fists
All the while listening
To the rush of the Gunnison
The voices of climbers in the distance
The sun sinks lower in the sky
The crickets and cicadas serenade us
We top out at the much-anticipated campground
Savor our cold cans of Lime-a- Ritas
While watching, the canyon turn from
Fuchsia, to gold
To black

ADVENTURES IN THE BLACK CANYON PART II

September 2, 2015

A pitch in rock climbing is a section of a route on a cliff that is climbed between two belay points, using a rope for protection from the dire effects of falling. (Google dictionary)

To belay is to fix a running rope around a cleat, pin, rock or other object to secure it. (Google dictionary)

WE HAD A LAZY SUNDAY MORNING. Everyone woke up tired, sore, and unmotivated to climb. We packed up our tents, sleeping bags, pillows, and sat around drinking coffee from the French press while debating what to climb. Sarah wanted to go big and Ariel didn't want to climb. I was indifferent, but thinking shorter and easier as it was almost ten and the weather called for a 40% chance of rain. As we mulled over our choices I could see Ben's desire to climb fading. We decided on Maiden Voyage, a three pitch 5.9 that Sarah had already done.

Maiden Voyage was known to be one of the shorter, easier routes in the canyon, but it's a long hike to get there. I thought that can't be too bad as long as we make it off the rock before the rain. Little did I know what long hike out meant! We took a second batch of pictures with our phones, saving the map, route, and description. We put on our harness filled with gear and

I slung the rope over my shoulder. Ariel and Ben promised to wave and take pictures from the lookout.

We stopped at the forest service to fill out a permit. If we don't come back for a few days, the rangers will start looking for us. Eighteen people have died in the Black Canyon since 1960 and I did not want to be another statistic. We left the white copy in the box and took the yellow copy, then headed down Cruise Gully to a static repel line. After two repels and a lot of poison ivy, we bushwhacked up a short way to the base of the climb.

Looking up, it did not seem half as terrifying as the repel down. Sarah racked up and put up the first two pitches* of the climb. The book said you could link one and two with a 60-meter rope. I put my hand in a dirty, wide crack to begin the climb. The quality of the holds got better as you reached the crux, a thin finger -sized corner to a chimney and belay* ledge. It is the most dangerous part of the climb. It was easy for Sarah, spicy for me.

Having most of the gear on my harness and with Sarah's encouragement, I took off to lead the third pitch.* Within one move, I lowered back down. For me, it is never lack of strength just lack of courage that sets me back. It was frustrating to have the ability. but be so scared. However, after switching the gear over to Sarah, and following her lead, I was glad I had not put up the pitch. Just like yesterday, the switch was fortuitous. The route ascended a wide crack and then a roof that I would have been terrified to lead.

Pitch* four was easy and we topped out at a great little rest and lunch spot. I was disappointed with my performance, but glad we did another climb. It was short and we were at the top and it was only 2pm. Little did I realize what lay ahead. Sarah ate smoked oysters and I ate PB&J. The trail out looked easy and quite obvious. I felt confident we would be out and safe before the weather arrived. As we turned the corner, my heart sank and my blood pressure rose. Below us was a descent full of routes and dead trees with The Gunnison River in view as a cushion should you make a wrong move.

Poor Sarah. I questioned her every move. Are you sure this is the trail? What if it is not? What if we lose our ground? How will we get out? I realized I was hurting and not helping the already precarious situation, so I took deep breaths and followed, gripping whatever I could find for security. We gave each other space not wanting to knock loose debris on each other's heads and finally arrived at a respite with terrifying exposure to the drop below.

Sarah looked around remaining calm and confident, trying to counterbalance my fear. Again, with assurance, she stated we are just below the trail; it is right there. She pointed to a smooth granite slab with an upside- down roof. Right there had never seemed so far away. A storm was building across the canyon and thunder threatened us in the background. Let's use a rope for safety, especially since you just have sneakers on. Great idea, I thought.

The ascent was smooth with few holds and prickle branches poking out everywhere. I held my breath not believing that anything was going to be easy after that last descent. I was brought up to worry and staying calm was not in my nature. While Sarah was thinking let's get out of here, I was thinking we are going to die, the river looks cold, and we will never get to eat chocolate again! Luckily, after a tough climb up never- been -climbed before rock, we reached a cairn and an obvious trail.

I was not ready to let down my guard until we had walked a bit and the path continued safely towards the car. Three switchbacks and a couple of yards we both smiled and celebrated that we were safe and going to make it back to the campground. The sky grew darker and the thunder louder, we walked faster, but were not scared anymore. We were on stable ground and headed in the right direction.

We walked past a couple of hikers waiting out the rain under the porch of the forest service and pushed our permit into the return box, happy to check off that we were back. Ben and Ariel had left. We threw our gear into the car relieved to take off the clanking gear. We jumped into the car just as the clouds let loose and the sky lit up yellow. What do you think makes us crave these adventures, we asked each other? We both decided we weren't sure, but these adventures remind you to be happy that you are alive. We giggled... so much for a short easy day!

PRE-CHEMO ROUND 6!!!

September 2, 2015

I HATE THE DAY BEFORE CHEMO. I feel like I have to fit everything in. I feel great and wish that the doctors would just leave me alone. I have been trying to eat everything while it tastes good. I have my day jam-packed with activities, but I am tired and just want to do nothing. I keep telling myself this is it. One more, make it through!!!

MY HERO AND ODE TO THE NURSES

September 3, 2015

COMMENTS

Sandor is quite the Grateful Dead fan. And I thank him for lending such a supporting hand, Just like the nurses who treated you so well. I thank them all for getting you through this hell.

Jen, Not as good as yours but it says how I feel. Congrats for getting to this point. Love, Cousin Mark
—Mark, September 4, 2015

MY HERO

Sandor
He is humble
He is strong
He is quick-witted
And he is kind
He smiles when I hurt
And is calm when I am not
He squeezes my hand
And sits all day patiently by my side
He questions what is important
And puts all else aside
To be with me
And hold me
And tell me
I'll be
Alright

ODE TO MY NURSES

Thanks to all the nurses
Who have lived through all my curses
Who have been here by my side
And stuck with me for the ride
To Leeza who from the start
Had a place close to my heart
She knew just what to say
To keep my fears at bay
She hugged me while I cried
And kept me occupied
To Kathy bubbly and fun
She reminded me it would soon be done
To Katie who answered all my questions
In our many pre-chemo sessions
She never told me no and never told me yes
She just told me be careful and do my very best
To Mari who checked my vitals and then took my weight
She always took the time to tell me I looked great
To Alec forever calm and arriving with a smile
He was continuously patient even if it took a while
To Margaret who was always there
With a great listening ear
She did not tell me what to do
And shared with me all that she knew
To Karen who came in late to Shaw
And learned what to do without a flaw
Thanks to all of you for always staying true
For helping to get me through
This crazy cancer journey

LAUREN

September 5, 2015

YEAH!! LAUREN IS HERE!! She left her baby daughter, Maggie, to come see me! I know it was hard, but I am so thankful to get some sister time and I think she is also getting some much needed sleep. Thank you Phil! I didn't make very many plans since I just had chemo on Thursday, but am holding up pretty well. It would be great if the weather would cooperate.

Today we squished in lunch at the Westside and a short hike, just before the rain. Got a little bit wet. We went to meet some friends for Friday Afternoon Club and then came home early. I got congratulations from people I didn't even know at the bar. It is funny what social media can do. All of a sudden, you have these friends you never knew you had.

I am hoping for some sun tomorrow so Lauren and I can go on a little hike and she can see how pretty Vail is in the summer. Then we get to go to Gourmet on the Gore, even though I can't really taste anything right now.

I am feeling pretty much like I did after my last chemo: dizzy, nauseous, achy, the chills, but relieved. It doesn't feel quite real yet. I thought there would be some exciting big shebang at the end of chemo, but I don't feel quite well enough to believe it is over. I am not sure if there will be a certain point of closure considering that what I have will never quite go away. Instead, life just might fade back into normalcy.

I had mixed emotions during the last chemo, aside from being sicker than I have been in the other treatments. I think it was a combination of being over it and having a lot going on emotionally right now. You get used to the routine and having to put your life on hold. It will be weird to have no excuses and no one checking in with appointments and follow-ups. Even after 6 months it still seems surreal that this has happened. It will be interesting to see what comes of this experience. Meanwhile, I am so glad to have my sister here to celebrate with me!

IS IT REALLY OVER?

September 8, 2015

IT IS HARD TO BELIEVE I am done. I don't know whether to celebrate, cry, or throw up. It doesn't seem real yet since I just had chemo. My head is still spinning and my body still aches. I also think I am programmed not to trust what I am told right away. since there were so many unknowns at the beginning. You don't want to get excited and then be let down.

This is going to sound crazy, but there is another challenge to being finished; what do I do next? Dealing with cancer and going to appointments has taken over the last six months of my life. It gave me a purpose though not a good one. I need a new goal, a good one. I know all of you reading this with kids and full time jobs are laughing as you would pay for five minutes of relaxation. However, for me, because I have been piecing jobs together and do not have family around, there will be a lot of empty time especially since I am still limited in what I can do.

In Vail, it is the mud season. It is rainy in the morning. Most of my clients and random jobs have disappeared. I usually substitute teach until ski school starts, but am not allowed to be around that many kids yet. I had planned a trip with Sandor, but I think he needs a Jen break. So I looked at my bucket list: get married (probably not going to happen), go climbing in Greece (need a partner), learn Spanish (doable). I am good at coming up with ideas, but not so good at the follow through.

I suppose, I just need to take one step at a time, get through this week and start feeling better. I need to get off the Prednisone, the worst drug in the world, and give my body a chance to feel better. I feel like I just ran a marathon and am finally getting to breathe, but I still don't believe it is over. Hopefully, as cancer moves from the front of my mind to the back, things will come together. Some new opportunity will present itself; it always does.

THANK YOU

THANK YOU EVERYONE for your support. I would like to dedicate this page to all of you who have been following my blog, who have sent me messages, cards, gifts, and most of all, supported me through this journey.

First, I would like to thank all of the nurses and doctors who got me through this process. Doctor Alec has listened patiently to my questions. Katie, who has done the same. Thank you Leeza for holding my hand while I cried and all of the other nurses who have cheered me on. I have been so lucky to have such a great medical crew.

I would like to thank my friends who have called, got me biking, climbing, and visited me in the hospital. You kept me going, made me laugh, and supported me when I cried. Thank you Heather and Christy for the hats. Sarah, Mia, Ben, and Chris for taking me to the rock, even on Percocet. John and Jason and Molly, my wonderful bike partners, I love you!

Thank you, Kelli for throwing me a party and keeping me employed when I needed work and Toni and Joe for listening relentlessly and giving me advice. Marty and Marly, thank you for always coming to chemo and bringing me caramels and gum. Thanks Sloan and Amy for understanding and sharing your experiences with me. You are two of the strongest ladies that I know. Kathleen, for your amazing advice.

Thank you, family, and friends for reading my blog. Aunts and Uncles, I appreciate your support: the calls, the gifts, and the responses. Mark and Lya, for my fabulous pajamas and Freshies. Betsy, for my Lulu Lemon sweatshirt. Jeff for all your medical advice and Terese for always checking in. Mike and Elizabeth thank you! Sam and Dan, I love my book and cozy hat and Becky,I love your emails! Thank you, Lynn, for your wonderful note.

Thank you, Mom and Dad, Laur and Phil, and Phil's parents. I have the cards stacked on my fireplace. Mom and Dad, I couldn't have done it without you. Thanks for staying positive as I know it must have been tough. Lauren, I loved having you visit and sending my care packages. I love my hat! Phil, it was great seeing you and Maggie on Facetime. Mom and Dad's friends, thank you for being there for them, and for your contributions to the Lymphoma Society. We will pray for a cure.

And most of all to the person who will never read this blog. Thank you from the bottom of my heart. I am blessed to have had you in my life during these challenging times. You cooked for me, came with me to every appointment, held me, and made me laugh when I cried. I can't imagine fighting this without you. I can't thank you enough. I hope you get everything that you want and deserve out of life.

POST CHEMO MINI VACATIONS

September 30, 2015

TWO WEEKS DONE. Will the fear dissipate or will I always be prepared to fight chemicals? Thank goodness for friends, campfires, climbing, and silly games. Biking, beer, and pizza too. All the little fun activities that keep your mind off of your problems. Six months of chemo. My counts still too low to teach. I guess I might as well go play!

A new start beginning with a bunch of mini vacations before teaching again. A week or two to deflate, have fun, appreciate being alive, and being done. I feel like I ran a marathon and I am finally able to rest, but my adrenaline is still going. First stop Crested Butte.

Crested Butte, a whirlwind three days. We drive over Cottonwood pass, yellow Aspens dotting the hills, and stop before the glass-still Taylor Park Reservoir. Biking Doctors Park with the boys, fun, smooth, fast single track. Racing to finish before dark. Dales Pale Ale and brick oven pizza before setting up tents by the bubbling Slate River.

Campfires and friends, smores, and dogs. 401 with Molly and her super great friends from work. Big jeep road climbs and steep uphill to Scofield Pass. Pictures and Gu and Cliff Bars. Exposed single track with cow ponds below. Manure on the trail and every once in a while, a cow too. Blue skies and twisting single track and rickety old bridges. More beer and pizza. An early night campfire and bed.

Paonia with Molly and Patrick. A quick strand ride in Crested Butte and then over Keblar Pass. Dusty water bars and hunters dotting the road. Paonia, a skip down 133, consisting of a block of wood houses that look as if they might blow over in a storm. Riding to the vineyards and tasting the sweet local grapes. The Stone Cottage, Azura. A buzz and peaches by the river.

Visiting Emily. A walk back into the sixties, how I imagined them. An earthship built from tires, off the grid with solar panels. Collecting water from the roof, raising goats, and growing kale. A sauna in a bus and a dance hall to sleep in. A night I will remember always. In the morning, a muddy, rainy ride. Hauling our clay caked bikes over our shoulders back to the car. Then back to Black Bridge for more wine.

Freedom. I drive fast on I70, the speed limit 80, once past the Colorado/Utah border. Singing Indigo Girls at the top of my lungs. No one, but me. Revisit my old CD's; Acoustic Junction, The Samples, Sean Colvin, Blues Travelers. A break from the Dead. Left at Crescent Junction and right at 500 Rd West. You know you are in Utah. Quick stop at the store. A hug for Mia at the Kings Bottom campground off Cane Creek Road. Bed.

Driving South past the Jailhouse Restaurant and the bike shops of Moab. The road, an interstate, flat and ugly until you reach the turn off to Indian

Creek. Stocked up with water and food for three days in the desert. I follow the camper reading Mt. Mia on the license plate. We turn right into the Canyonlands. The flat desert road beginning to spiral through willows, past newspaper rock, then through the slowly rising Windgate Towers standing majestically along the road peering in at us.

An afternoon hike up to the wall and trial by fire for Jen. No mercy with Mia who has made climbing her life. A fiery blond Swede, who dresses in pink, and has all the boys wishing they could climb like her. A little sympathy for the cancer, but not much for my lack of crack climbing abilities. I watch her ease up the rock, hand after hand, foot after foot. Listening to her advice. I struggle, sweat, and curse, and not as gracefully make it to the top. Relieved to have the sunset, we make our way down to the campground for some much needed food and rest.

The guides from Moab Cliffs and Canyoneering are two spaces down. We eat left-overs and mac and cheese and join them by the fire. I am reminded of my age, as I learn the game Whiskey Slap. They shake their heads when I mention quarters. Giggles and laughs later, I curl into my bed in the back of my car, preparing to get beat up by Mia again the next day.

Two days and 9 climbs later, I am relieved Mia has to work. Her patience in taping my hands and throwing in a 5.10 or two (rare find at the Creek) has saved my skin, but not my strength. Her young friend, Mary, inspired me to keep persevering, but after trying to ring lock a 5.12 splitter crack and trying to send a 5.11+, technicolor, in the dark, my juice is gone. A day on my bike, a shower, and warm bed, high on my list.

I swooped into Vail, used the bathroom at City Market, a camper's dream, then headed to ride Captain Ahab. Two flats later and some good company from two people I met on the trail, I arrived at the car with a broken derailleur. A sign it was time to head home. A stop at Kohls in Grand Junction, a limeade for the ride, and some more old CD's. What a great way to end the trip. Just what the doctor ordered, along with no more chemo!

Distractions are great, but coming home and facing life is a necessary evil. Much easier to do after a mini vacation. A few days of teaching and figuring essentials out and I think I will take another mini-vacation. I figure two mini vacations equal one big one and really there is nothing more important in life than enjoying it!

CHAPTER TWO
CONFRONTING

November 2, 2015

COMMENTS

Pinkus! Keep on keeping on! Chin up, throw some serious attitude at the big C and take it DOWN. You have so much love being town your way—we are sending up prayers for you and your family. Endure, absorb the support and love, and hopefully this will all be behind you soon.

    —Lisa, November 4, 2015

This news is crushing, but from what you've already gone through, you can definitely get through this as well. Stay strong and know you have a ton of people pulling for you!! Much love.

    —Jeannie, November 4, 2015

Jen, as I opened your latest post I expected to read about some new adventure, maybe that the rights to your journal entries had been purchased or maybe that you conquered another climbing first. Like all I am in disbelief and saddened by the thought of you having to endure more treatments. Why is it that bad things happen to such good people. Kick some more ass and keep your chin up...the world is behind you. Big hug?

    —Your buddy, Nate,
      November 3, 2015

This news is a punch in the stomach but it is not the whole story. As a medical social worker I have seen how again and again a temporary re-visit to the original diagnosis is sometimes harder to take emotionally after all seems to be 100% ok. And thankfully so often

I CANNOT BELIEVE I am writing again, as I was sure that my story was complete. I finished my last round of chemo and took off to climb, bike, and go to Mexico. I returned feeling strong and healthy and ready to celebrate conquering lymphoma. As it turns out, one cell was stronger than the others and has resisted the chemo and is continuing to grow rapidly in my body. This all seems surreal to me as my hair is growing back, my bones are feeling better, and the only pain I have is in my lower back. I never ever thought that I would have to face the steps that will follow.

I met with my oncologist in Denver this morning. My cousin Jeff and Sandor accompanied me. I could not have done this without them and feel truly blessed to have them in my life. It was decided that I will have a biopsy this week. I will then begin two rounds of a stronger chemo that will be administered over a four -day period. I will remain in the hospital for these treatments. I will begin taking Nuelasta shots to release my bone marrow into my blood stream. They will then collect my blood for a stem cell transplant. Another two rounds of an even stronger chemo will follow with a three week stay in the hospital, where they will replace my hopefully clean cells.

I am angry, frustrated, disappointed, and scared. This is something you read about in books, not something that really happens. I am in the process of deciding whether to do all of this in Philadelphia or Denver and am trying to figure out insurance plans. It is all overwhelming and tricky, and logistics make it hard to stay positive. I want to take care of everything and play while I am still able. Yet, having fun is a real challenge right now.

I apologize for continuing to bug you with my life. Please take me off your list if you do not want to read more. I understand this is not light reading. I will not be offended, as I am writing as much for me as I am for you. I do thank you for your continuing support as I step out to battle one more time.

that re-visit turns out to be an annoying (albeit scary) blip. May it be this. Your poetic gift, Jen, reminds us to celebrate the HERE and NOW. Also the strengths, the laughter, the sheer goodness of who-you-are and the gifts you bring to each challenge and each relationship. You're an easy person to love, and your postings have been love letters to the world and awesome lessons in living.

—Baylee, November 3, 2015

IF I DIE

If I die
Please celebrate
Spread my ashes
Over the Aspens and the ski slopes
Smile as you remember
All the good times we have spent together
Laugh at the bad ones
And forgive my weaknesses
But appreciate my strengths
Hug each other
And be good to one another
And think of me
When you ride Son of Middle
Ski WFO and Seldom
Or climb at Homestake
I will be watching and
Wishing I was there too

DATES

November 4, 2015

DEAR EVERYONE,

Thanks for your support and desire to help. I am overwhelmed with logistics right now. What will be most helpful is if you can look over these dates and continue to send me cards, flowers, funny pictures, food during the weeks that look rough. Help Sandor and my family get through but understand if we are too busy to be social. I will keep you posted on whether I am in Denver, Vail, or Pennsylvania. If I do not get back to you please know that all your love and support is keeping me fighting.

This is a letter from the clinical nurse coordinator at U. of Co. Cancer Center with a timeline for treatment:

Dear Jen,

LOGISTICS:
I did not put any dates on the timeline since we are not exactly sure when you will be starting your "treatment" based on getting your 2nd opinion. Dr. K. does say the latest she would want you to start treatment (RDHAP) would be 11/16, so I will write out a tentative timeline for transplant so you know approximate dates.

- C1 RDHAP starting 11/16 – 4 days inpatient at UCH
- C2 RDHAP starting 12/7 – 4 days inpatient at UCH (can get work-up tests done during inpatient stay)
- During post chemo follow-up appointments in our clinic, we can have you meet with our team members (psych, dietician, MD who oversees stem cell collection)
- Plan for PET, BMBx to be around 12/21
- Plan to start 4 days of neupogen (to grow # of stem cells), Friday 1/1/2016.
- Collect stem cells starting Tuesday 1/5/16 (plan to be here 1/4-1/8)
- Plan to admit for RBEAM treatment and transplant 1/19.
- Transplant admission is around 3 weeks long, so discharge would be around 2/9.
- Plan to stay within 30 minutes of hospital from 2/9-2/23.

If you do plan to stay locally for this whole process (2 cycles of treatment, stem cell collection, and stem cell transplant), I would plan for about 3.5 months stay in the Aurora/Denver area.

This is a LOT of information in one day, so please refer to this email when needed and do not hesitate to ask any questions via email or phone. As this process progresses, and we get closer to planning your work-up meetings, then collection, etc. I will be in touch a lot and educating you along the way. I will meet with you when inpatient here to go over the collection process again, and then when here for collection, I will meet with you to discuss what your transplant admission will be like, etc. So I'm here to educate and assist the entire time. I'm glad Cathy our SW met with you today as getting grant money would be beneficial.

NEXT STEPS:
Shauna (RN Coordinator) is working to get your biopsy scheduled. I am working to get your Oct PET scan read by our Radiologists (needs to happen first before biopsy can be scheduled).

Do you have dates you are going to UPenn?

Hang in there! We have a great team to help you get through this! Kate

CREEPING UP QUICKLY

November 5, 2015

IT IS CRAZY HOW ONE DAY you can feel fine and the next so ill. I guess it is like the weather in Colorado. I can feel the change. My gut was sore but now it is on fire, sending electric shocks throughout my body. Thank goodness for Percocet and Tylenol. A great combination. The good P as opposed to Prednisone.

I am still in shock that this is happening to me. I fought RCHOP so well. I biked, I climbed, and worked through it all. I am starting to wonder if my body is too strong and nothing can kill off the invaders. Maybe I exercise too much. There is no other reason that I can conclude why the cancer came back.

I have gone over all the things that I have done wrong in life. There are many. I complain about little things that are not worth it. I'm stressed by decisions that mean very little and am constantly wishing that I was better at everything that I do. I have major envy of everyone who is cute, young, and healthy right now. I compare myself to cancer fighters and wonder what I have done wrong and wonder how they have made their cancer go away.

In life, it seems like often the results go with the effort. With cancer, I find the results are not turning out to depend on anything that I do. I feel like I have no control. You read about the fighters who conquer the disease. You hear about how strong and amazing they are to live through such a battle. But, you never hear about how strong those who die are when they probably fought just as hard if not harder than those who live.

I am not used to putting in a lot of effort and losing. This is new to me and I find it incredibly frustrating. I do not understand how the torture of going through chemo could not have ended in positive scans. I do not understand how a fairly young, active person who was living a pretty normal life could have it flipped in the course of a day. I don't understand not having any control over what to do next.

I am not a good decision maker and these are hard decisions. I hope I am making the right ones as it is hard to keep faith in the medical field when you get results like I have.

Don't give up! Don't blame yourself or anything you did or didn't do on your current crappy circumstance! Cancer is a strange being. If there were straight forward answers as to why some people beat the odds while others fall on bad luck such as yourself, the medical people would know by now.

Why do some hardened alcoholics live til they are 85? Why do some daily bacon eaters never have health issues? Why are some kids violently allergic to peanuts while other kids can eat an open days old Milky Way off the counter?

We aren't computers that get plugged in and evaluated and fixed. We are oddly developed beings who occasionally run into difficult to fix problems.

Your good spirits and strong mind are what you have control of. Don't let go of that control. Stay strong and positive, your body will follow as best it can.

Bad luck sucks, but there isn't a damn thing you can do beyond picking yourself back up and staying in the fight. You know you have 1000s of people backing you and sending as much good energy your way possible. We are here for you and will continue to support you however possible. In the words of Courtney G FU CANCER!
—Kelli, November 5, 2015

I was thinking about the same thing —you are the strongest, healthiest person I know, and I don't think there is a 'what did I do wrong' answer. It does seem unfair, but I suppose that's what makes cancer the crappiest of sicknesses: it can hit anyone. Yet, after your 6th round of chemo, when you were supposed to be knocked down, I had trouble keeping up with you on our hike! I think that because you are so tough, you'll be one of those people that conquers this. We haven't lost yet! I love you and look forward to you kicking my butt on another 10 mile hike!
—Lauren, November 5, 2015

Hang in there, Jen. There are many people thinking about you and praying for you. We all know you are fighting hard. If you're up to it, read Stuart Scott's Every Day I Fight. And hold on to your faith and love of life.
—Jill, November 5, 2015

FUCK THE WORLD AND MORE POEMS

November 9, 2015

COMMENTS

Hi Jen,
What woman with such life force (as you have)...wouldn't be angry in this situation? Understandable with all you are dealing with. Although I was warned to "never" to write the F word publicly, I would do anything to "flip this poem" for you (the beautiful girl next door). So here is a try.... Remember "Fuck" rhymes with Luck and Pluck. Wishing you much Luck and Pluck in this next treatment chapter. Each chapter has a new path... be open to discovery and recovery. Please add us to your cheering section. With love, Ruth and Barry
    —Ruth, November 9, 2017

The world would be very empty without you in it. So let's flip that poem and focus on a healthy and happy future. We will be there to support you!
    —Toni, November 9, 2015

I think you mean make love to the world because the other line is from another girl I think it's Jennifer the name on the patient manifest not the one who loves this world and never can rest but the one who listens to all the doctors and their sad stories instead of the one who revels in her glories fat tires on singletrack plugging gear into sandstone cracks going cool places wearing packs dropping off cookies and cards to her friends that's the woman we all call JEN recognize the love that swirls around you like a tidal wave sweeping away your worry family, friends, students all playmates ready to play again with JEN

FUCK THE WORLD

And all of its false promises It's a sore back
A hernia Cancer!
But the good kind of cancer Hodgkins Lymphoma
You kill it and it goes away
Oops
Its Non Hodgkins
But still an 8 out of 10
You'll have RCHOP
Well tolerated
You'll fight this
Scans are 98% clear
Good job Jen, you're amazing
Like I had anything to do with it
Almost in the clear
But
No that one cell
It is still there and growing
No worries
We'll double the chemo
Take all of your blood
Kill you and then
Bring you back to life
There is a 50-60 percent chance this will work
And if not you'll die poisoned and in the hospital
Alternative medicine will not help
You start on the 16th
Dr. G. from Mexico says
Your family and friends do not support
My science based solution
You have had chemo
I cannot help you
You are not ready for m
Denver doc says your choice is Philly or Denver
Not Mexico
If you wait it will be too late
Dr. G says if you have chemo
It will be too late
No one listens to me To my questions
No one gives me a better option
No one says I will be OK
But if I pray Go to church
Have faith in God
I will be saved
I will win

As if I am
A failure if I die
Doesn't seem like a fair game
Fuck the World
And God if there is one
Because he/she is not a good God
He wouldn't do this to a
Healthy 41 year old
Someone please
Flip this poem
Squelch my anger
And give me
The will to live
And peace
Instead of Anger

I LOVE YOU FROM THE SKY

Mom and Dad and Lauren, Maggie, and Phil
I want you to know
That I am trying to have the will
But should I not
I want you to know
That I love you more
Than words can show
If I should die
I have lived a good life
Full of joy and happiness
And little strife
There is nothing
That you or I could do
Death is not because of me
And not because of you
I will try my best to build up my might
So that I can put up a good fight
But if I lose
I want you to know
That I love you so
Please cry but then smile
It may take a while
Spend time together
Forget about sorrow
You never know
What might happen tomorrow

who smiles back at the sun and scowls at the rain and still goes out to run this race is new the track is bumpy the grade is steep your dignity is inside you it can't be taken only given away so hang on tight you made it to another day a day in a life well lived

—Joe, November 9, 2015

STRIPPED OF MY DIGNITY

In March I was Strong Confident
Excited for the summer Healthy
Making decisions about Life
Jobs friends activities I was Me
Talking about everyday things I was pretty
Now I am weak
I talk about cancer
I read studies
And talk to doctors
And take Percocet I am shy
And scared
I want to curl
Up in a ball
I am ugly and bald
Stressed out Nervous

LOGISTICS

Please make sure
My house goes to my family
Sandor included
Please make sure my ashes
Are spread on bike and ski trails
And to my Mom and Dad
Please make sure to help
My family be happy
Please make sure you do not fight
Please make sure if there is extra money
It helps kids climb, bike, and fight cancer
Please support your selves with it first
Please remember me with fond memories
Tell stories and laugh and smile
And know that I love you

SCHEDULE AND APOLOGY

November 10, 2015

NOT VERY POETIC and kind of rough but I guess that is how I have been feeling lately. Sorry, to be so open with my thoughts as I forget how widespread social media is. Needless, to say it has been a rough week. Maybe, someone can edit this someday for other patients and make it more reader friendly.

I am posting my tentative schedule one more time, as many people have called and asked how to help. A friend is setting up a dinner thing for post chemo week. Otherwise, I will be at my house, Sandor's, or the hospital. As far as visiting goes please feel free to stop by after chemo, but understand if I am not always great company. I never know how I will feel.

Keep checking my journals as I might have to go to Philadelphia for the transplant in January but will keep you posted.

Thanks again you guys are amazing!!!!

COMMENTS

Never apologize. Your poems are beautiful and moving, and most importantly the raw truth of what you are feeling. Let it all out—dump it on us and let us all help you carry the burden. XO
　　—Natalie, November 10, 2015

Marshall and I have been—and continue to be—grateful for the honesty and humanity (and yes, the poetry) of your postings. It is a privilege to be part of such a large, caring circle of friends and relatives who are learning along with the life-lessons you share with amazing grace. In a world that skims the surface, your openness is a gift.as is your way with words. Keep posting and we'll keep learning.
　　—Baylee, November 10, 2015

Hi Jen, We know you are suffering, and you have the ability to express yourself in words. Better to get it out, and not keep it bottled up. Just through the darkness, remember there a lot of folks pulling for your and you are an incredibly strong woman. Love YA
　　—DAD, November 10, 2015

SWEPT AWAY

November 11, 2015

COMMENTS

Jen, when I read your poems, I laugh, I cry, I feel inspired to live life and not sweat the little things. You are a warrior showing your true colors.
  —Your buddy Nate,
    November 17, 2015

Great, great writing. You're in the thick of it. I've always wondered about the black and white, martial metaphors that get used when people have cancer, like "fight", "battle", "victory", "brave", "hero" etc. It seems like they're one-sided pink-ribbon words that make other people around the person feel better, but not always the person who actually is deal-ing with the disease every day (kind of like combat veterans— they mostly don't feel like heroes). Do those words imply that if you're not fighting every minute, you're being weak? That if you say you're scared and angry, you're not being a "hero"? That if you lose the "battle" and die, you somehow failed?

I saw in my mom's case that war-riorship in the face of a life-threatening disease has a lot more nuance. She passed in 1974 due to cancer after three bouts. She didn't succumb and "lose the battle" and she was NOT a failure. She met her life and walked her path fully, head on, and opened her lionheart to all of it, fear, grief, death, pain, life and love. That's warriorship, walking the hard path with full, open attention.

That's what I see you doing. I hope this makes sense. Love and hugs.
  —Joanne, November 11, 2015

BEGGING FOR THE PAST

I look around the room
And beg to have that old feeling
Of just planning for the next day.
What to wear.
What school I will be teaching at
What the kids will be like
I beg for the time
When I could plan the next adventure
And giggle over silly little things
When biopsies were a big deal
And Percocet was against my belief
I beg for the day when
I was stressed over fitting in all my activities
Not fitting in time to research whether I will live or die
I beg for the days when

I didn't know what it was like to be jealous of a clean scan
And compared myself to who had on a cute outfit
Not to who has hair and who is healthy
I beg for the day when friends came over to come over
To celebrate have fun
Not to be with me before chemo or to help support me
Because I am too stressed to help myself I beg for the day when
I could sleep through the night
When my stomach didn't tighten and my heart didn't clench
When my body was at ease
And my mind was at rest
And the background was yellow
Purple, blue, and green
Not grey or black or
Streaked with crazy
Electric colored lines

SWEPT AWAY

Swept away for a moment I am holding baby Jackson
Thinking about life and little tiny hands
Thinking about being a mom a dad
Bringing a whole new meaning into your life

Swept away for a moment I am hiking The North Trail
My Dansko's getting clogged with mud
Sharing hopes and dreams with my college friend
Laughing over how pricy are diapers and car bills

Swept away for a moment
We are deciding what wine to drink
Where to put out the appetizers
And which sushi to try first

Swept away for a moment
I listen to the buzz in the room I climbed ruins in Indian Creek
Ran a half marathon in Moab
Swept away for a moment

We talk about moving to San Francisco
Share old iphone climbing photos
And talk about banana cream pie

Swept away for a moment life feels less serious lighter more fun
Like what it used to be and should still be
When I didn't have to hold my breath

When my parents could go out and enjoy the night
When my sister could be with her baby
And laugh with me not worry about me
Not facetime me because they might not get to anymore

When I could sweat the little things
Because there were no big things to sweat
When my mind was at ease
And my heart was smiling

Thank you friends For the chance
To be swept away
Even if just for the night

IT CAN'T BE REAL

This is what you see in a movie A book
Not what happens to me
When I sleep it is not real
When I play I forget
But then I wake up
The doctor calls Emails
Hugs and tears from friends
It is so real
It is like a war
Is about to happen
A history book coming to life
One that other people survived
And others did not
And now I am being forced into battle
Like "The Fault in Our Stars"
"The Diary of Anne Frank"
The heros you read about
And then are thankful
They are alive and
That you are not them
I will have to pretend
"Life is Beautiful"
And I am in a science experiment
That will save future lives
Keep it fun like Roberto Bernini
Flip reality but how
I just want to sleep
And pretend this is not true

THE BUTTERFLY LADY

November 13, 2015

STAGES OF LIFE

I believe I was always a dreamer as a kid
Maybe everyone was
Maybe not
I pictured flying through the clouds
And lying in fields of flowers
Singing on stage
And dressing in gowns
As I got older the visions changed
I pictured
Whole Foods and yoga
Saving kids in Africa
Organic vegetables and lotion
Hiking to the tops of big mountains
At thirty yet again to
Owning a log home with barnwood sides
A perfect husband three children
A dog
But then I became pragmatic
I do not know if it was due to age
Or to life experiences
I could not Omm at yoga anymore
And organic seemed expensive
A condo made more sense
And a dog too much work
At 40 Cancer took over
I poured through articles and books
Refused to eat or use the microwave
Read about
Kale, carrot juice and coffee enemas
Meditation yoga and frankincense
Round two
My pragmatic side
Chemo Percocet and Ibuprofen
But the dreamer comes back
And I opt for both
Chemo Percocet
Yoga and massage
And the Butterfly Lady

THE BUTTERFLY LADY

A small room Tucked away
She asks me to tell her
My story in my own words
She listens speaks softly
I lie on her table
Staring up at cloth butterflies
A ukulele or flute plays
The lights are off
She walks me through life
A 7-year-old memory
Flatsy dolls
Michelle and Michael
Lauren's curls
Big beach balls
Fear
Let go of the fear
She spins my feet
Tests my strength
Then at 15
GFS trying to fit in
Eating alone writing poetry
Worrying
Good thoughts she says
She spins my feet
Tests my strength Now 35
Wanting kids, dating Sandor
A hodge podge of jobs Stress
Drop that she says
She spins my feet
Tests my strength
Reframe your story
You are not alone
You are not the only kid that
Feels fear stress and worry
You are worthy
To be a part of the whole
Picture your disease Greens purples
Flowing away from your body
Release the stress
Forgive yourself
She spins my feet
Tests my strength
The butterflies watch
And strangely
I am stronger

WHAT I BELIEVE

I believe
In Westernized Medicine
But I believe
In mind over matter
And that I need help from all of you
And traditional medicine
And myself to
Fight along
With the chemicals
Please help me
To stay strong
And keep fighting

HELP

November 16, 2015

COMMENTS

We're all right there with you. Positive thoughts, lots of love, thinking of you, visualizing a very healthy future. You're one step closer.
　　—Mark, November 16, 2015

You've got this! And you have tons of people who have your back who are sending you all those things and more. XOXOXO
　　—Natalie, Matt and Ashley,
　　　November 16, 2015

PLEASE GOD HELP ME TO BE STRONG.

Room 1134 Inpatient building 1 11th floor
M-Th

Positive thoughts,
distraction,
love,
visualization,
hope,
belief,
courage

A MAZE
OF CORDS

November 17, 2015

COMMENTS

Jen, you are a kindred soul...your strength, enthusiasm and optimism are an inspiration to one and all. There will be many powder days ahead and ice falls to climb. Hugs & prayers
 —Nate G, November 18, 2015

Dear Jen, I read your amazing and intuitive posts all the time, with laughter, with tears, with anger at the cancer, with wonderment at the strength you have, with tears for your struggle. I decided that I had to let you know that you have another person pulling for you.
 —Judith, November 17, 2015

We feel your strength here in Pittsburgh. And also the love connecting you to so many folks from all over this land. We're looking out that snow-covered window with you. Just as we're with you as those cords do their jobs. Each of your postings has brought us into your strength and your capacity to so beautifully share that strength. You'll get back to that fluffy powder on Prima --victorious. (Looking forward to reading your poem about THAT adventure!)
 —Baylee and Marshall,
  November 17, 2015

THERE IS A MAZE OF CORDS

One is connected to the chemotherapy
One to the saline solution
Another to the master plug that sits next to
The one that attaches to the heating pad
And the stand that reads my vitals every fifteen minutes
Last night I was 117/80 pulse 68
126.4lbs and this morning 130.9
Too many liquids
To the right is life
A big white window covered with snow
So thick that you cannot see where the plains meet the mountains
Or the line of cars piled up on I70 trying to get to work
Or even the fluorescent sign that says University Hospital
My drip gurgles as it releases this new cocktail
Stronger than the last guaranteed to kill that one bad cell
My mom breaths deeply on the pull- out couch positioned under life
I can feel the chemicals pour into my veins
Blowing up the bulk of the tumor that remains
I am weak and nauseous
But I know all these cords are doing their jobs
I feel the love and the good vibes sent to me from all over
And pray that these cords that trap me
Will be the same ones that allow me
To return to the fluffy powder on Prima
And the large icicles forming in East Vail
And the wonderful friends and family
That are getting me through this Maze of cords

UPS AND DOWNS

November 18, 2015

UPS AND DOWNS

I was super sleepy and now I am super wired
I was super skinny and now I am fat with liquid
I was super calm but the Oxycodone has worn off
I was super-hot but now I am super- cold
I was surrounded by love and now I am all alone
I was super healthy but now I am super sick
I was super psyched on life and now I am super down
I was super sure the doctors knew everything and now I am not so sure
I did believe in faith and I am not sure I do anymore
I do believe I must be brave and put up a good fight
But I used to be super strong and now I am not.

HOSPITAL ROOM

The board in my room says my name, Jen
The nurses who will help me Julia and Katelyn
It says my weight and who will support me
And the date and goals for the day
Yet it is 11:30 and there are no goals
Written on the chart
Nor has a nurse come to visit me
Thank goodness for my mom and dad
And the friends that came to visit
They got me out of my bed
And distracted me from my thoughts
Please let tomorrow be the same and make the liquid drip fast
Don't let me have the time to think
And please write me a goal.

COMMENTS

I read your heartfelt poems, and it is awesome that you use writing to help heal your spirit, when you don't have the opportunity to heal your soul with athletics. I sort of know about these lines, fluids, noises, fear and loneliness you write about at night. Not from experience, but from caring for others. When friends and most of the hospital staff have left for the night, you are there, with your drips and your thoughts. Having been a nightwalker once, I know these nightwalkers in the hospital are there for you, reach out to them if you need to talk or a hand to hold, or even just a reassuring presence in the room. They will reach back!

The Chaplains have some of the greatest gifts to give you! They offer hugs, are active listeners, and just beautiful, amazing people to be around. Talk to them about fear, anxiety, hopes and dreams...they are seriously some of my favorite coworkers in the hospital and my guess is will give you warm fuzzies at some point too!

I love all your friends and family after reading these posts! Your warm, giving, gentle spirit attracts all of these phenomenal people! Good juju from all over the country, near and far. This juju, in my opinion , has equal importance in the healing process as the physical medications.

So many hugs to you my friend! Let's play again soon when you are feeling up to it and hope to see you on the 18th. (or the next week or two in Vail) xxoo, Much good juju to you!
—Erica, November 18, 2015

Cords suck Drugs suck
Being a medical experience suck
You will always be a friend
You will always be a smile
You will always be someone to play with
I will always be here for you
I love you GF and
I'm looking forward to getting after it
again XO
      —Mia, November 18, 2015

TO MY FRIENDS

I do not know how you hold your head up high
How you march across the water
How you smile and pat my back
And say it's going to be OK
When I feel like a walking experiment
Where I catch a person's eye
And not so they can say hi
So they can change my fluid
Get me food or help me to the bathroom
I used to be a friend, a smile
A person to play with
And you who have been through worse and longer
Call me up and say Buck up
Stay strong
I don't want to hear you looking for pity
Close your ears
Don't listen for the beeping pumps Sweet dreams
Happy thoughts
I am strong you say
You amaze me with your power
We are all pretty amazing you say.

MINI UPDATE AND LAST NIGHT'S DREAM

November 22, 2015

I OWE YOU A MINI UPDATE but have been too sick to eat, drink, or sleep. I never thought that my life could change so drastically in three days. I am slowly recovering thanks to my mom who has bathed me, read to me, and held me tight and my dad who has been the fearless warrior planning, and arranging, and hugging me. Thanks to my friends for all their support. It warms me up to get your texts and see your smiling faces. I am trying to make lists of what I am grateful for and appreciate all the little things that I often take for granted. I am hoping that I can learn from this experience. One day at a time.

LAST NIGHT'S DREAM/YELLOW SALT HILLS

Get up, get up, it is a very important day
I've discovered an enema that will work I say
It will bring back the good and make the bad go away!
Get up and get ready you have to prepare
It is all very timely and the hour is near!
You have to change your DNA it's like taking a pill
But first you must ride to the top of Dr. Seuss Hill
You will know it, it's yellow with white piles of salt
Make sure you get up and get a very early start
I will prepare what it is that you will need to eat
Don't be surprised if it is not very sweet
There will be Barbie doll hair and horse hooves that we'll grind
The Manning van will pick you up at a quarter past nine
You must leave them your blankets as they zip down the road
Then Chip will be there with the others I am told
It might not taste pretty or sit very right
But then the bad juju will be out of sight
So, go to the hills where the salt looks like snow
I've got your best interest in mind as you know
In the end there will be a small Enstrom's Square
It will change your DNA and then I'll be near
Go quick I say there must be no delay
I will hold you tomorrow it will be a brand-new day

THINK WHITE

I see the bags and hear the beeps
Think white
The red lights flashing liquid inside Think white
My belly gurgles, I am parched
But not thirsty
Think white It is still dark
When will night end Think white
But then it will be tomorrow
A day closer to having to do this all over again
Think white

ANOTHER THANKS AND FLIP FLOP

November 26, 2015

AS YOU KNOW WRITING IS MY OUTLET and it is crazy that my energy has been too low to even write. I am going to have to get savvy with my new computer, as I bet there is a way that I could dictate to it. Maybe a Siri Write? Let me know if you invent it.

I know I am constantly giving thanks. But it is appropriate now and once again needed. To my family and sister and the BIGGEST THANKS to you ALL. I know everyone says not to worry about responding and due to my brain and the amazing number of people that have been supporting me, I am sure I will forget to thank someone. But, please know I am feeling and appreciating all your support.

Last week was by far the hardest week of my life. I never imagined it was possible to be that sick. I feel like I have been to war and back and I survived because of your love. The emails, texts, gifts, and food have been overwhelming and so helpful for both me and my family. Really, though, the most important aspect for me has been knowing you all care and are keeping me in your thoughts. reminding me to be positive, to fight, and to want to survive.

I believe in science, but I also believe in the power of our minds to turn situations around and make them bearable and help us fight to live. Like the movie, A Beautiful Life, sometimes you have to flip flop the situation. Honestly, that has been the hardest part because there is so much fear involved in this and so much that is unknown. And when you are stuck in the hospital sick and alone and your body feels like it has no more to give, you need to have something to hold onto to keep afloat.

All your stories and wishes and pictures of fun are keeping me going. Today my friend told me about a person she knows who battled with cancer. When she was told she had a 95% chance of dying, she said that she was glad she wasn't going to be a part of that number. I am going to keep that story in the front of my mind and keep fighting my hardest to stay positive and alive.

Your messages and warm wishes continue to push me on. Thank you.

FLIP FLOP

Queen of Spades Ace of Hearts
In the sun In the dark Flip Flop
Cracker Jacks Chuckles candy It is awful
It is dandy Flip Flop City lights
Mountain quiet It is peaceful It's a riot
Flip Flop
Cold and brittle
Soft fur blanket I will die
I will make it Flip flop
Red suede slippers Patent leather
Hard and stiff Light as a feather Flip Flop
Gold and Yellow Sea or Shore Wind or weather Flip Flop

I KNOW HOW THE KIDS FEEL

(Jen taught at a school for children with physical and mental differences)

Please hug the kids and the parents together
All of the students that I taught for so long
Who continue to fight on
Wake up
Come to school
Despite that their heads might be spinning
Their guts turning inside
Knowing that the drugs are the only thing keeping them alive
Hug all the teachers and their friends at school
For helping them to continue to make it through
I know for them now every day is a battle
And credit them for their will to survive Today and here after

FAMILY PHOTO

November 26, 2015

Thank you my family for being here.
Words can't express how much I love you!!

POEMS

Indeed.....
Strong cells are waiting for the right
moment to pop up.... Indeed.....
There are so many strong cells
Some haven't arrived yet, but they are
enroute.... Some will come your way
from crazy places like Rifle, East Vail and
Moab.... Don't fret..... They are on the
way!!!!
    —Mia, November 26, 2015

I am glad to read your powerful writings
of yesterday and today. We will visualize
this return of strong cells, and send
you our love. Please hug your family for
us. We are glad you are surrounded by
family and friends.
    —Love, Judy and Robin,
     November 26, 2015

YOU BEING YOU AND ME BEING ME

It is crazy to think that just a month ago
I was working, climbing, biking in Mexico
And now I am hopeful to just make it for a walk
I can't go to work because my blood counts are too low
I might need an infusion on Friday
And I wake up to a cocktail of anti-this and anti-that
Swallow the pills, then take an Oxycodone for the pain
I see this in movies or maybe retirement homes
But not for me the healthiest person I know
I can't go to restaurants, Walmart, or the grocery
No bars or parties and skiing is out
Work could be dangerous and certain foods too
Everything that makes me, me and you, you
On the flip side
I have my wonderful family and friends
A home that is pretty and a river to walk to
I can take lots of pictures and video chat
Have good books to read, a computer to write on
Visions of skiing, snowshoeing, and climbing
And Yak Traks in case I can go for a hike
I have the hope that this will be a bad stage I will go through
And hopefully I will be back to
You being you and me being me

VISUALIZATION

The cancer it is grey and mealy like waffles
It floats in my lower left abdomen
It is broken into pieces and is soft and very weak
It shreds and disintegrates and breaks into pieces
The chemo floods my body in waves of yellow and orange
And attacks all the grey each and every last piece
My kidneys are running
My heart is beating and all the good cells strong and healthy and alive
Now comes my army of white cells in large numbers
Fish with strong teeth filling every part of my being
Here to protect me as my body is healing
Back in full swing
My blood clean
Running smoothly
Ready to kick into gear
To go hiking, to go skiing, to be on the hill with the wind and fresh air
And my family and friends
So dear no more grey only
Red cells and white cells and me being everything that I always wanted to be

CATCH UP / THANKSGIVING WEEK

November 29, 2015

COMMENTS

So happy to know it was a family filled holiday!! And the awesome thing about writing...it's always there when you decide you want to come back to it :-) XOXOXOXO
　　—Lynn, December 2, 2015

God bless you charming Jen whom we admire for your wonderful gift of grace in all your movement and even in your trials. So glad you are walking and doing what you love. xo
　　—Helaine, December 1, 2015

Great news that you've been out hiking and feel like you have a short break from this horrible ordeal. It sounds like you have tons of support and are surrounded by a good team of people who love you and can hold you tight and help you get through all of this. Just wish you didn't have to ... XOXO
　　—Natalie, Matt and Ashley, November 30, 2015

So good to spend time with you Jen, and your family. Jen, you make a difference in my life. Thank you.
　　—Rebecca, November 30, 2015

CATCH UP ON TODAY AND THE LAST FEW WEEKS

For some reason
I have been uninspired to write
It has kind of been a whirlwind of chaos the last few weeks
And sleeping and trying to read silly books has been my reprieve
For some reason typing just wasn't working for me

I definitely feel like I went to Iraq and back
Don't remember most of chemo week
Lost lots of weight and feel pretty weak

I was so lucky to have family come to town
It was good, but emotional
How else could it be
When everyone loves each other so much.

We took care of logistics
And everyone helped to revamp my house
I now have cable, internet, clean curtains, a new rug
A beautiful Christmas cactus and lights that work in the kitchen

Mom, Dad, Laura, Barb, Becky and I all at my house
We ate, we hiked, we shopped, and had tea
Everyone left me today around one
The house is quiet and actually quite nice

I am feeling much better and hiked with some friends
My blood counts are low and my platelets are down
But John came by for dinner and I watched football next door
And tomorrow I'll hike with Sarah and Mia and more

So despite all the awfulness there is a short break
To eat lots of food and get some fresh air
To reorganize and catch up on things
And feel like myself and try to block all the fear.

Thanks once again Mom, Dad, Laura
And all of you for the great cards, gifts, and wishes you've sent
My fireplace is lined with wishes and care
My bathroom stocked with bubble baths, soaps, and creams
I am so grateful to have such a wonderful life!!!

LEAVING VAIL

December 3, 2015

I wish I didn't have to wake up as it is so much easier to be asleep and not think about my life.

However, I have had a fun, healthy week. I have skinned, skied, ice -climbed, shopped and had Mexican food with a great crew of friends. Once again cramming everything in before I am sick again. What a crazy way to live life. Unfortunately, along with my fun has come a very hard decision. I was originally planning to move to Philly in January and finish this round of chemo there. However, we were having trouble making the move and staying on schedule so that, if all goes well, I can be a candidate for a T-cell transplant *(a fairly new procedure at Hospital of the U. of Pa.). To my surprise, the doctor in Philly emailed me on Monday with a solution. I will move to Philly now so Dr. N. can meet me and we can maintain the medical protocol that was started.

It has been hard on me to wrap my brain around having another month here with my friends and Vail family to moving in three days. However, I know that it will be much easier on my family (who are my caretakers). The commute back and forth to Denver for chemo, along with finding housing, and my parents not knowing anyone here has been a real challenge.

I will be missing my friends and sport outlets that keep me healthy and distracted. Vail friends you have been wonderful at keeping me busy, skinning, climbing, taking me to dinner. Please continue to Facebook me, text me, email me, Facetime me. Your love is helping send me energy and power to fight this. Philly friends if you are around come visit me. Take me for walks, distract me. Mom's friends, I look forward to learning Mahjong.

Meanwhile, I want to give my family hero status for making this all work. It has been more than complicated getting records, insurance, and communicating with the doctors to make this happen. Aside from the stress of the whole situation, my parents and sister have remained supportive, relatively calm, and are fighting for me to have the best care and support possible. I am so lucky to have such a wonderful family. Please support them in this process. Thanks to my cousin Dr. Jeff and Sandor too who have been great mediators and sounding boards through these hard decisions.

*A T-cell transplant is where bone marrow cells are harvested from the donor and manipulated in a lab to remove cancerous cells. The remaining healthy cells, including blood forming cells, are infused into the patient. (Google dictionary)

WHILE I'M SICK

December 8, 2015

Thanks you friends and family for all of your support as I transition to Philadelphia. I arrived to both my mom and dad at the airport to pick me up. They are being amazingly strong through all of this. We visited Aunt Helaine and Uncle Jack, ate cheesesteaks, and watched The Voice. I am hoping to go for a long walk. I go into the hospital today at 1pm for my second round of RDHAP Chemo. Open to calls, emails, and visits if I am physically capable. I have posted the dates and location on my planner. I will have more details about the building and the room this afternoon. You are all wonderful! Make your day wonderful too! Every day is precious!

WHILE I AM SICK

While I am sick
Ski Seldom and Wedges
Ski Over Yonder and WFO
Skin up Meadow Mountain Geneva and Simba too
While I am sick
Go skate ski up Sandstone East Vail and Tigawon Rd
Go ice climb at Pumphouse The Fang and The Des
While I am sick
Be with your friends
Laugh with them, eat with them, call your family,
Mom and dad hug your kids and husbands
While I am sick
Be grateful for your job
If you are skiing with my clients
Take them down Hairbag, Powerline, and Coyote Escape
Don't burn out on The Magic Forrest
While I am sick appreciate your health, those who surround you,
The mountains, the snow, the creeks, and the oak trees.
While I am sick
Smile and have fun
Don't sweat the small stuff
And enjoy all of the good
Life is short

NIGHTMARE DAY

December 9, 2015

YESTERDAY DID NOT GO WELL. We met with the doctor at U. of Penn. She was very nice and reassuring. But the hospital is big and everything took a long time. When we finally got to the inpatient chemo ward there was a guy with a posse of policemen in the room next to me. Apparently, he was escorted here from jail. Then they told me it was going to be hours before they could begin the chemo. So, we went to dinner only to come back to be told that they did not have the consent form to start my chemo. In fact, they cannot even get the consent form without an oncologist and they have all gone home for the night. It is now 7:30 and I have spent the day in the hospital but not had any treatment.

My anxiety has been shooting up over the last few days and I have been frustrated and angry. Luckily, my parents are wonderful. They brought a spin bike into my room and are staying as positive as possible under the circumstances. It still seems surreal even though it is happening to me as I write. It also seems unreal because I am so functional between chemo treatments. It is hard to let them make you sick when you feel just fine. It is hard to believe you are sick when you have only been healthy and done everything right. How can they not know the cause? How can this be happening?

What do I need is mostly distractions; however, it is hard when the doctors come in all the time and decisions have to be made. It is hard when you don't know what you can do or who you can see, because you don't know how you are going to feel.

My parents will never say yes to help but keep them busy and check in with them, as you have been doing, because this is hard.

Thank you.

COMMENTS

Hi Jenny,
What a miserable start to your stay at Penn, at least you have the spinning bike. Start riding. When you get to the other side of this nightmare you'll come to LA and we'll ride to San Diego. Just think about 11 hours of riding down the coast. Can't wait.
      Take care. And I'll check in on your parents. Love,
      —Mark, December 10, 2015

What you have written -with honesty and integrity--is a message that should... no,must....be communicated to someone on staff. An ombudsman, perhaps. Or a social worker. As you know so well, the point of being in the hospital is to get better, not sicker. As patients we are so often afraid to speak up. But we must. Not only to report complaints but to let those in charge of care (at every level) understand your fears. The #1 rule is RESPECT FOR THE PATIENT as an individual rather than as a diagnosis. PATIENTS MUST COME FIRST! (Health care professionals know this but sometimes need to be reminded.) You are a fine writer. Ideally your caregivers need to be educated as to how glitches in scheduling , etc. can make a tough situation torturous, .
      Keep telling your story... good people will listen. Distraction? Write a manual for caregivers: "Dear Doctor..." By the way, Jen. Your good sense and resilience are amazing. Truly.
      —Baylee and Marshall,
        December 9, 2015

CHANGE

December 10, 2015

COMMENTS

Jen,

I have said it before and I will say it again, you are amazing. A light snow is falling tonight and I thought of you as I took a quiet walk. Your words don't sweat the small stuff, hug your kids, enjoy your work and live each day!. They Resonate with how you have always lived your life for at least the 23 years I have known you. Continue to keep your chin up. You, your writing and your sheer determination are an inspiration to everyone who knows you. Big hug,

    —Nate, December 14, 2015

The yellow mask brings out the color of your eyes! I'm sure all your creativity is total entertainment for the hospital staff. Keep up the positive energy and funny antics. You are a CHAMP!!

    —Kelli, December 11, 2015

I love your writing, it is so creative and funny and also full of meaning and encouragement . Looking forward to walking with you in the woods, doing yoga and playing mahjong, after they spring you out!

    —Judith, December 11, 2015

CHANGE

Change is hard
But comparing is no use She has a new Lexus
I have a beat- up Subaru
He gets paid twice as much
I work my ass off and make half
She is so skinny and she never works out
I have to get chemo to get skinny
He is so good with directions
I get lost wherever I go
She is healthy and having her third baby
I am stuck in the hospital with lymphoma
They break all the rules and take advantage of the system
I am the goody two shoes who does everything right
She has beautiful long brown hair
Mine is about to fall out again
But I am funny and creative
I am athletic and stoic
I work hard at what I do And I am taking a hit
For everyone else who is healthy
Comparing doesn't help
You are given the hand you are dealt
So the choice is to deal with it
Hopefully you wouldnt be given more than you can handle
I believe it to be true
I believe it to be true
I believe it to be true

FLIPPIN' IT AROUND /HOSPITAL AT UNIVERSITY OF PA.

Like my poem Flip Flop I had to make a change
Last night was rough
This morning I was super sick I slept until 1pm
But then I made up for it Mom and I went for a hike
We stopped and flirted with the policeman guarding the sick prisoner in room 204
Then we stopped and visited Jorge at the far end of the wing
Ironically he used to landscape for us
When our basement caught on fire
He saved our house and called the fire department
Mom and Jorge gossiped about family
I got to practice my Spanish
Then we headed north and switch- backed to the left
Some nurses overheard me say I was from Colorado
Everyone joined in with their ski stories
One even offered to do yoga with me
And told me there were alternatives to downward dog

Thank goodness upside down might not work right now
We hiked past the final rooms before mine 2006
Peeking in but not wanting to disturb
Wondering if there were people my age
If there were people who had been here a day a night a week a month
Were they having transplants or just chemo
Then past the rubberband man
Who leaves me rubberbands to try to shoot into the bin
Across the office and behind the desk
He says I do more laps than anyone who has ever been in the ward
And then adds that I make him dizzy
I tell him I am gonna start a board
And have a competition for the most laps
And the winner gets a new pair of sneakers
He asks if he has to do it
It is hard to be in a new place
New people new hallways to hike
Not everyone is blond and wearing Patagonia
But it is what you make of it

AFTERSHOCK AND EATING LIFE CEREAL AT HOME

December 14, 2015
Philadelphia Home

COMMENTS

Thank you for your transparency. Not only is it wonderful to get a glimpse of how you feel (and others) but it's such a reality check to appreciate our health, friends and the good in our life, and conversely learn from you how to tackle positively what you are facing. Your victory is the world's victory so know that you are thought of and being rooted on big time! Rock on girl!
　　—Melinda, December 14, 2015

How many chemo patients take a 3-mile walk the day after chemo. At least Mom and Dad had their exercise for the day on Sunday. Each day will get better and better.
　　—DAD, December 14, 2015

SORRY

Once again I have been uninspired to write.
I think I needed some time to digest the culture shock
And the PTSD that has occurred in the course of a week.

My condition has been unpredictable.
However, I am free from the wires and the drips and the beeps.
No more police roaming the hallways.
I can walk more than the diamond square that circles the unit
No more vitals or thermometers in the middle of the night.
No midnight blood tests or measuring my weight.
I can pee and shower without calling a nurse.

Despite all that I was glad to stay an extra night in the hospital
As my condition was and remains a bit unstable.

I find it hard to describe the aftershock of chemo.
It is a flu, but no flu that you would ever want.
I feel like I sailed around the world twice at record speed in a tornado.
My head is full of fluid, my brain is spinning, and everything echoes.
Food tastes bad, but not having food in my mouth tastes worst.
Standing makes me dizzy, but lying down makes me even dizzier.

Emotionally, I am either wired on steroids like Dexamethasone
Or drugged on Compazine and Ativan and can hardly keep my eyes open.
I can listen to one person talk, but not two because I hear echoes.
I am focusing on what you are saying, but most of the time thinking
I hope that I make it through this conversation without getting sick.

However, each day is a little better and a little brighter.
And each morning I check and am excited that I am still alive.
I am becoming used to waking up to birds and trees at my parent's house,
A pleasant solace from the semis on the I70 corridor.
I am loving having Mom and Dad spoil me and check in on my every move
And sitting in the sunny kitchen and eating Life cereal with Sandor.
Together we light the Chanukah candles at night.
The 72 degree weather is pleasant for a walk in the Wissahicken,
Even though I keep getting overly prepared with long underwear and a puff jacket.

I miss the snow and being surrounded by mountains.
I hung pictures of my friends in my room.
Kelli keeps me updated on Facebook and email.
My AMAZING friends send me unlimited glimpses into their lives: their hikes,
Christmas tree excursions, weddings, and parties.
It makes me feel like I am there with them.

My family, parents, friends have been wonderful,
But I have not really been up for visitors quit yet.
Soup, rice pudding, and lasagna have arrived at the house.
My aunt and sister bought me all kinds of pajamas.
Friends from childhood and Sandor's friends from Philly have called to
Check–up on me.

It is amazing what your body can endure
And how supportive people are in times of need.
We underestimate the power our minds have over our situations and how
Important it is to discipline yourself to think in a positive way.

I was doing my laps in the hospital the other day.
I would do 5 laps and write a quote on the wall.
Then switch directions, do five laps and write a quote on the wall.
I was very picky about the quotes.
There are so many clichés and I find them frustrating under the circumstances.

However, here are the two that I put up on the wall:
I believe in living today. Not yesterday, nor tomorrow.
Life is 10%what happens to you and 90% how you react to it.

PTSD

December 14, 2015

I am feeling much better and love being with Mom and Dad. They are taking good care of me! This is how I feel at night, when I look at a hospital, or think or hear of any of these chemicals.

PTSD

Drip drop, split splat
Twist, twist
Beep
Flash green, flash red
Bright black strobe
Saline Benadryl
Dexamethasone
Cytoxan Cisplatin
Soap
Paper pillow, rough sheets
Dry skin
Itch
Drip drop, split splat
Twist, twist
Beep beep beep
Flash twist aghh

PRAYER

December 15, 2015

A PRAYER

A blood orange globe rises between
The pines and oaks
It burns through my childhood window
As it did when I was 6
18 and now 40
But this time with new meaning
It comes with a prayer
Dear Chemotherapy,
Please radiate throughout my veins and lymphocytes
Spread your beams and eradicate all weak mutant cells
That have replicated and taken over my body
Do not stop until you have poisoned every last particle
Stomp on every last piece
Burn every flake until you have scorched all remnants
Overlook nothing
Be scrupulous
Then make room for only the good
Let them return with caution
Then allow them to flow freely
But do not allow them to stray from their original form
They should work together in harmony
Pump clean blood through my body
Create armies of white blood cells to recognize and fight off the enemies
But do not allow the enemies to return
Surely after being scorched they will never dare
And let the blood orange sun rise again
Amen

BREATHING

December 16, 2015

BREATHING

I have been breathing
As I go to the gym with my dad
And watch him do his daily workout
Out with the negative in with the positive
I have been breathing
As I walk the Wissahickon with Mom
And her wonderful and supportive friends
Out with the negative in with the positive
I have been breathing
As I go to DSW and Target
My favorite stores to go with Mom
Out with the negative in with the positive
I have been breathing
As I listen to Mom's Mahjong group giggle
Over wine and fruit and chocolate
Out with the negative in with the positive
I have been breathing
As I stretch to the sky and salute the sun
As I reach to the earth and spread my hands
Out with the negative in with the positive
I have been breathing
As I sink into the hot steamy bath
And the pain disappears if just for a while
Out with the negative in with the positive
I have been breathing
As you shower me with unconditional
Kindness, love and support
I have been breathing
Out with the negative in with the positive.

ALONE BEFORE THE SCANS

December 23, 2015

THE NIGHT BEFORE THE SCANS. Can't sleep. Worried about me and my family. Don't understand how everyone who walks by me, that is on TV, that is on the radio is fine and I am not. Don't understand how people who have lived half as healthy lives as me are not sick and I am. Can't figure out what I did wrong. Can't stay calm. How do you stay calm under these circumstances? Suggestions???? Looking for some calm. Don't know how to find it.

ALONE

Anything else in life friends can relate to
You break up with a boyfriend
You get all kinds of advice
It will suck but it will get better
You have to move
It will be a pain and a lot of work
You will have to get adjusted to the change
But it will get better
You lose your job
Could be for the better or the worse
Might be tough for a while
But it will get better
You have surgery
Puts a damper on life for a bit
But then you will mend
And it will get better
You have cancer
And no one can relate
You have chemo and it doesn't work
You have to go for scans
And the result will be either bad or worse
No one can relate
And no one tells you it will get better
I have so much more to do
It is not fair

NO MORE TEARS

No more tears No more crying
No more tension in the room
It is time for happiness
For my heart to relax
It is time for a break from all this foreign talk
Time to smile to laugh over silly things
To plan vacations and eat to eat not because I have to
It is time to pamper Lauren and Maggie and Phil
And run on the beach with no worries
Carefree
Light

WHILE YOU'RE OUT SKIING

December 24, 2015

MY SCANS WERE NOT CLEAR YESTERDAY. My cancer is not responding to the chemo. I will not have another round of chemo or a transplant. They will discuss what my other options are. Most will be studies and we will have to hope that one works. I guess I will be in Philadelphia indefinitely. Meanwhile, we are working on getting a second opinion in New York.

It has been a very stressful day for everyone. We are not sure how to live with this knowledge and how to put it aside to function on a daily basis. It still seems surreal. I don't feel like it could possibly be happening to me. It is easier to be in denial as facing it is too scary. How do you not wonder what you did to make this happen and what you can do to make it go away?

A worst nightmare coming true.........How do you deal with it?

WHILE YOU'RE OUT SKIING

While you are out skiing powder
I am being given radioactive injections
While you are heading down yonder
I head into the PETSCAN machine
While you are eating wings at Moe's
I am consulting with Dr. N and my nurse
While you are drinking a beer
I am swallowing steroids to keep the pain away
While you are clomping back to your house in boots
I am leaving UPENN for the 100th time
While you are making dinner
I am praying that something in the fridge will look appealing
While you are laughing with your family
There is a pit inside of my stomach
And inside of my mom's and my dad's
While you are hearing about your kids' days
And planning tomorrow
We are thinking this cannot be happening
And please let there be a cure
While you are crawling into bed
And dozing off into a good night sleep
I am tossing and turning
And hoping to sleep because
It is a better alternative than thinking

Please allow my parents space and time to process this. I have not called anyone as it is easier not to talk about my situation right now and to just stay busy. Thanks for your understanding.

NEW YEAR

January 1, 2016

HAPPY NEW YEAR

A little brick restaurant
A cross between modern
And country Italian
Long wooden tables
Bottles of wine
Pinot, Malbec, Chardonnay
Dishes like Eggplant Parmigiana
Meatballs and peppers wrapped in prosciutto
Not too fancy, but just right
Tucked away amongst
The row houses of Conshohocken
Loud, but not too loud
Enough to feel like you have company
But allow you to still have a conversation
Giggles from one end of the table
Wine glasses clinking from the other
To old memories and new
Old friendships and new ones
Additional family members
And new travel stories
A lovely tradition of good friends
Celebrating and toasting to another year
Good people who I want to protect my family
To help them get through this next year
But I know it is not their fight
A fight that is always easier with friends
And maybe this will be a better new year

HANGING ON TO HOPE

January 4, 2016

I GO TO THE DOCTOR TODAY. None of us slept well last night. I was up. My mom was up. I heard my dad tossing and turning. Jeff, my doctor cousin, is coming. That will be helpful. I am terrified. My parents too. They have been amazing through this whole process.

We spent the weekend with Lauren, Phil, and Maggie. I got to see Mike, Elizabeth, and the kids. It was good to be busy and to get to hug everyone. I am trying to be in the moment, but it is hard. However, I really wanted to get to hug as many family members as I could in the last few weeks before hearing what my next steps will be. DC friends be good to my rock star little sister. Maggie, I love you!

Again, I am so grateful for all my parent's friends and my friends who have taken me to dinner, on walks, and kept me distracted from my life. I am not the best company, but you are keeping me going. That goes to my friends far away, who are doing all you can from a distance. I wish words and love could fix everything. I keep hoping I can have one more week of playing in Colorado and hug you all too.

It is not fair that I have to live on a schedule and think these thoughts. I have so many more important things to do. I want to be working, skiing, eating burgers and fries, and watching the Broncos with Sandor. Doing what a 41 year old should be doing. Not choosing between bad and worse.

HANGING ON TO HOPE

Thank God for my family
Reminding me to hang on to hope
Dad always optimistic
Mom continuing to be her loving self
Lauren the glue holding it all together
Hanging on to hope
At the top of Long's Peak
Stuck for the night
No warm clothes
Only a rope a harness
An electric storm and us
But there was hope
In Israel where
The Arabs and the Jews
Have fought
A continuous battle
And keep fighting
There is hope
In New Orleans
Where homes got flooded
Restaurants leveled
Lives taken and livelihoods destroyed

COMMENTS

Jenny hang on to hope!! There is so much more climbing, biking, aunting, daughtering, friending, living to be done. Praying for good news from you next appointments. Sending tons of love and good wishes from NY.
　　—Lynn, January 5, 2016

Your poem resonated in ways I can scarcely articulate. And your rumination on being precariously perched on the edge of a precipice hit every button perfectly. All of us keep you and your family in our thoughts.
　　—Susan, January 4, 2016

Keep hanging on to hope as tight as you can when it gets hard. Your poetry is so poignant and each and every one of them touches and inspires me. You are an amazing woman. XO
　　—Natalie, Matt and Ashley,
　　　January 4, 2016

You are an amazing Aunt!! Maggie loves her aunt Jenny! We will help you fight and hold on to hope!!
　　—Lauren, January 4, 2016

There is hope
In New York
Where buildings got toppled
Offices in flames
Loved ones died
And America wounded
There was hope
In Lymphoma
Where the last 6 months
I have battled and
Fought and been sick
There are new cures
And new therapies
There is hope
When the night is dark
And the stars are out
And you think no
Shooting star will fall
One falls
Out of the Corner
Of your eye

PARALYZED BY LIFE

I am paralyzed by my diagnosis, by my inability to fix what is wrong with me, by my lack of control over the situation and by not understanding what I did or did not do to make this happen and that no one knows the answer.

If I do nothing, I have a few months to live. If I do something, I could die anyway.

If I get more drugs, I will be sick. They may work or they may not work.

If I do nothing, I could die drug free but the cancer will take over my organs and stop all my body parts from working.

I will suffer either way.

Do I die at home?

Do I die in Vail?

Do I die at UPENN?

How do you make decisions you never thought you would have to make?

Where does your money go, your home, your belongings? How do you want to be buried?

Will you jinx yourself if you answer these questions?

Why do my parents have to live through this?

It is not fair.

They are such good people.

I have so much to do;

So many friends to see, activities to finish.

It is time for me to be working, playing, aunting, not time for me to be paralyzed by life.

TRAIN WRECK

January 5, 2016

So, for those of you wondering, I met with the doctor. We decided chemo is not working for me. She gave me two medicines that are immunomodulators to try. One is Lenalidomide, another is Nivolumab and Pembrolizumab combined. They are pills or IV's taken every few weeks. The hope is that my cancer will respond by either remaining the same or shrinking, but that one of the two choices will at least stop its growth. If this happens they can get me into a T-Cell immunotherapy trial that will hopefully put the cancer in remission. We are waiting to see which drug insurance covers and heard that Nivolumab has a higher chance of working.

We are also going to a New York Hospital on Friday to get a second opinion and see if there are any trials that are recommended that we didn't hear about. They also may be able to give us some insight as to if one drug is better than the other. It has been a long and hard few days, full of lots of information and more hard decisions.

I thank you again for all your support as always. I have gotten a million wonderful texts and letters and feel so loved. I know it is helping me get through this process and helping my parents too. Hopefully, we will make a choice by next week. It would be great to get the cancer to respond and stop spreading and make me hurt. Thank you for reading and understanding if I don't get on the phone to explain the story again. It is hard to repeat.

TRAIN WRECK

My body went from this mecca of health
To this broken train wreck that keeps getting run into
I look at the pile of trials my dad has copied
And pop another Oxycodone into my mouth
Dessert to go with the Cipro, Fluconazole and Senna
I can't believe my life of teaching, skiing, laughing
Has turned into a series of doctors' appointments
And drugs with names I cannot pronounce
Like Lenalidomide and Nivolumab
Ones that you hear the commercials for on TV
And swear that you will never take
I roll under the covers with my hoodie and hat
I can't seem to stay warm at 116 lbs.
And listen to my dad repeat my story
On the phone again
I know it helps him to help me
But I think at some point his brain is going
To need a break so I take it for him
Putting the articles aside and choosing
To type a poem and check my Facebook instead
I did my research this morning

And will do it again tomorrow afternoon
And then again, all day Friday at Sloan Kettering
I do not know if more people and more advice
Are the answers
I think the answer
Has been given and it is now up to my body
To respond
My mecca of Colorado health
Needs to pick its wrecked self back up
And get into gear and be reminded
What is healthy to have grown inside of it
And what is not
Please let one of these drugs be the answer
So that I can go back to being me
And piece my parts back together

SNOW, SNOW, AND MORE SNOW!!

January 21, 2016

It has been a while, but a justified while. I was told that I had a last week to travel, so I packed up my pajamas and an otherwise empty suitcase to bring to Vail and booked a ticket to fly to the mountains on the 12th. It was a last minute $1,000 ticket. Thank goodness for frequent flyer miles. They were the best used miles ever. Whatever higher spirit is up there has not been looking out for me but he/she sure did this weekend.

I arrived on time for Sandor to pick me up and give me a quick hug. I wanted the long hold-me-tight one, but, I guess you get what you get. We cruised back to Vail on empty highways and dry roads, a good treat for this time of the year. The morning was rough as always, shooting pain up my side and major constipation. This is what has made me not write for so long. The pain has definitely been growing more intense.

However, the skiing, friends, and company eased the pain. I had a good sunny Sandor ski day on Wednesday and then a hike up Meadow Mountain with my girlfriends and Kreston. Thanks Kreston for coming along and waiting while I did my belly flop flail position to ease the pain every 200 or so vertical feet.

I got to have dinner with Marly, Kurt, Kelli, Kreston, Sandor, Toni, Erica, Bo, and Christy, all my favorite people at my favorite restaurant Nozawa. Couldn't be better! I spent Friday packing which was really stressful as I could not decide what to bring to Philadelphia and what to leave here. I am still having trouble believing that I will not be in Vail this summer.

Friday afternoon was tough as I just couldn't seem to get rid of the pain. Every time it went away, it came back. I would take a hot bath and it would come back. I would take Oxycodone and it would come back. I would drink a Margarita and it would come back. Finally, it just resulted in my curling up in a ball and falling asleep.

Saturday was equally as difficult in the morning. I feel like I have to plan to leave an hour in the morning to try to go to the bathroom and even that doesn't work a lot of the time. However, once I risked leaving the house with Mia, it was a fabulous 6-7-inch powder day. A perfect day for skiing the Minturn Mile and the Saloon was open!!! Yeah!!

I was surprised to be surrounded by all of my favorite Vail people. I told a few people I would be there, but had no idea it would be such a fabulous and wonderful afternoon. Christy was in her "I Love Pinkus" top and Victoria came with Avivah. We had a great Minturn crew and then a great taco margarita crew. It was everything I pictured and more because we had 15 inches of new snow.

A final powder day to top off my amazing week and then a win for the Broncos. What more could a girl want (maybe to get better). It made up for being sent to hospital in New York for the week, well maybe.

STAYING
AWAKE

January 22, 2016

DEAR GOD,

If there is some lesson I need to learn, please help me to know what it is. I will work hard to learn it, I promise. If there is some lesson I am teaching others, please make sure I am really helping a lot of people, as you put me through this. If there is something I am doing wrong, tell me what it is and I will apologize and try to make it better.

Please give me some peace. Let me have the life that I once had back. I will not take it for granted and I am sorry if I ever did. I will be more compassionate, more giving, and try my best not to allow the Jewish guilt to kick in. I will learn to be more laid back, to relax and to have fun. I will strive not to compare or be competitive, but to be kinder and a better team player.

You always hear how amazing this person survived cancer and is now running a marathon. Or, how that person fought colon cancer and is now riding a century. You never hear about the person who relapsed, then transformed, relapsed again, all the while going to the gym and fighting just to get up in the morning and walk around the block.

Or how today just staying awake in between the Oxycodone and the Oxymorphine to write this has been a feat! You never hear about the people that fight it and die. They might not win the battle, but that doesn't mean that they did not fight or were not tough. Maybe they just had more to overcome. I hope there is some prayer in life for them, as dying with it is as hard, if not harder, than beating it.

PAIN, PAIN, AND MORE PAIN

January 22, 2016

I KNOW EVERYONE LOVES NYC but so far it has brought me pain, pain, and more pain. The appointment was for 9. We left Philly at 6, got there at 9:30. A little different than 75mph along the I70 corridor. Instead of lots of snow, there were lots of tunnels, bridges, and beeping NYC drivers with apple-red faces. My dad starting to blend in with them.

As we wove between lanes twisting in and out of Central Park, I curled up in the back seat, biting on my lip to stop from moaning. It helps for a while and then we hit a bump and it all goes straight to my left hip. I absorb the radiating throb and brace myself for the next 6 blocks towards 12th and York.

We reach the garage and I crawl into the elevator praying that Dr. G. can give me something to relieve the pain. My poor parents have listened to me groan the whole way up. They have been kind and comforting and tried to help take my brain off the pain. Dad parked the car and Mom takes me up to the lower lobby.

Just making it there is a feat, all the doctors and nurses rushed over to help me. I am grateful. It was definitely embarrassing, but it got me my own room and some stronger Oxycodine. It also got me admitted to the hospital for the week. As much as I wanted to go home, this was a good thing.

I have a great woman named Deb as a roommate who has been helpful and full of good Sloan Kettering advice. I really like my most recent nurse Bryn. She is going snowboarding in Vermont next week! Although, I still hurt, the pain is helping me figure out what drugs will best help relieve the pain and the constipation.

I also think it is easier on my parents, as I hate for them to see me in pain, but I can't hide it because it just hurts too much. It has been a process to get me off the drip and onto pills and I still am not sure if I am getting the right dosage to make me feel better.

But, I can walk around the unit without crawling on the floor, can pee without assistance, and know I am surrounded by help if I need it. I even looked out the window this morning and the skyline turned from a musty grey to a clear blue sky. Maybe NYC is not so bad.

COMMENTS

So appreciate your honest and detailed reports. Your writing takes my breath away...thank you! Love to you and your parents.
        —Susan, January 22, 2016

Jen, I'm only a second away!! I'm with you in spirit and energy 100% of the way. With a #flatpinkus in my pocket rest assured you are getting out. Luv ya
        —Mia, January 22, 2016

Jen, we are only 30 min away to your north if there is anything you or your parents need while you are in the city. Sloan Kettering is an amazing place that cured my brother-in law's cancer after a very bad initial diagnosis! Lots of love and strength to you all! Xoxo
        —Allyson, January 22, 2016

TRIALS

DEAR JEN,

Here are the trial suggestions for those of you who are science savvy. Do not feel obligated to read them. They are long and complicated. I chose the first study with Nivolumab and a drug called Ibrutinib (something like that). Feel free to read or trash the email or just let it sit, because it could give you headache.

The trials recommended to you at MSK are interesting. All three explore immune drugs, which are designed to activate the immune system in different ways. Three of the four trials that I have selected for you are also exploring immune checkpoint drugs; the one with CAR-T cells could be "saved" for future, if needed. So, there is an agreement in this regard - preference to immune system activating drugs. The only difference is that MSK suggested trials that are running in MSK, and the trials I have selected are in other locations on East Coast. Here is the short info on MSK trials:

https://clinicaltrials.gov/ct2/show/NCT02253992

This trial combines two drugs activating immune system, and I would rank it highly. The first drug in the trial, Nivolumab, had an overall response rate of 36% in a different trial, as a single agent. There is hope that addition of the second drug will boost the responses.

https://clinicaltrials.gov/ct2/show/NCT02454270

This test, a drug of a new type that literally brings together cancer B cells and immune T cells, for destruction of cancer cells. The drugs is in very early stage of testing, and there are no results yet, even preliminary. It looks very promising, but it's also very new and the drugs has no record of activity.

https://clinicaltrials.gov/ct2/show/NCT01953692

This is a trial that continues testing of a single immune drug, pembrolizumab (Keytruda). This drug is very similar to Nivolumab, and will work for probably about one-third of patients with DLBCL, same as Nivolumab. For this reason, I would not choose this trial. If you enroll in a trial, it makes much more sense to choose one that combines two drugs, because this might have a much better chance of working. This is the main thrust of many trials of immune drugs like Nivolumab and Keytruda – combining them with other drugs that have different mechanism of action seems to be highly promising.

Please keep in mind is that by consulting at MSK, or any other clinical center, you are limited in to the trials that are conducted there only. There is nothing wrong with this, but there could be more exciting trials elsewhere.

From the trials that I have selected, obviously from ct.gov, I would suggest that at least two are likely to be more promising than any of the trials above, mostly because each of the four drugs in these two trials is an already "known entities", and produced good results:

https://clinicaltrials.gov/ct2/show/NCT02327078

This trial combines Nivolumab with another drug that has been shown to give a further boost to immune system, enabling a better attack on cancer cells. This is considered to be a highly promising combination, and both drugs, as I mentioned, have a record of activity in cancer. In Columbia U, NY.

https://clinicaltrials.gov/ct2/show/NCT02220842

Combines two immune drugs in different categories. Both drugs in this trial have a record of activity in DLBCL, and their combination could work really well. In NY, NJ.

Trial with ibrutinib in my short list (https://clinicaltrials.gov/ct2/show/NCT02401048) could be relevant if DLBCL is of a certain type, known as ABC. This subtype responds much better to ibrutinib than the other subtype known as GCD. Analysis of mutations at MSK will determine, hopefully, which type Jen's DLBCL is.

Please let me know if you have any questions; I will be glad to answer.

Best regards, Emma

PARTY FOR PINKUS

HI ALL—
This is Jen's sister posting on behalf of Jen's amazing and wonderful friends in Vail. You guys have huge hearts!!

Jen's friends are holding a Party for Pinkus!!!

JEN PINKUS- SWEETEST ATHLETE IN VAIL

PARTY 4 PINKUS

Please join us
TUESDAY, 1 MARCH
Route 6 Café
6 pm
to celebrate and raise funds for JEN

$20 donation
includes one beer, one raffle ticket and apps

SILENT AUCTION, LIVE MUSIC AND RAFFLE PRIZES

Grand raffle drawing at 8! Win a 3 night holiday at Beaver Creek, breakfast included, dinner at The Golden Eagle and The Dusty Boot (winner does not need to be present)

For additional raffle tickets, donations or more information, please call kelli on 970 390 9145

HARDEST DAY OF MY LIFE

February 22, 2016

SORRY THAT I HAVE BEEN UNABLE to get back to people; it has been a rough month. I am now receiving radiation and getting steroids to shrink the tumors. My left leg is very weak. I don't have a lot of energy. I am surrounded by my family who are here to support me.

I still love all of the cards and photos and gifts but I am too weak to respond. I never knew how quickly my life could be flipped around so I appreciate each moment. I truly appreciate all you have done for the party. I would love to be there on Skype, but do not know if that will be physically possible. I will be there in heart and spirit.

I'm in New York now, but will probably be in Philadelphia after this week.

Sending love.

*so you can get back to the mountains
and be the badass that you are known
to be!*

    —Becca, December 25, 2015

*Jen, just want you to know that Salle and
I, and little Siggi & Bodi are thinking of
you! S&B are looking forward to when
you can give them ski lessons some day
soon! (After all, they probably won't
listen to their dad.) So don't forget who
took you climbing the first time!! ;-) Love,
Siggi, Bodi, Sallie and Jim*

    —Jim, February 22, 2016

*Jen! Wow! What an event tonight! Just
wanted to tell you my thoughts as I left
Route 6..... "That was the HEART of the
valley! YOU are the heart!" So many
different walks of life and different
periods of your life! You are amazing!
Keep your head up. Love, Liz*

    —Liz, March 1, 2016

*Dearest Jen,
If there is anyone who will be able to
overcome this is you.... I have yet to see
a mountain you cannot climb up to later
ski down, a bike path you cannot ride or
a day without one of your smiles. This
world, and my family, in particular, is
better because you have been a part of
it. We are with you every step of the way.
You have shown us love and dedication
and we can only see you get the same
from us. Much much love Emilio, Sharon,
Emilio, Hannah and Mauricio Azcárraga*

    —Sharon, May 13, 2015

*Dear Jen,
You are one of the most beautiful people
I know! (And when I say beautiful I mean
it in ALL the facets of your life) so you
are going to look beautiful any way you
are, or any color wig you choose! Please
remember we are always here with you!*

    —Sofia, May 16, 2015

Jennifer Erin Pinkus

May 9, 1974 - March 18, 2016

A Memorial was held for Jennifer Erin Pinkus at Donovan Pavilion on Thursday, June 23 at 6:00 p.m.

JENNIFER "JEN" PINKUS WAS BORN on May 9th, 1974 to loving and very excited parents, Ralph and Cheryl Pinkus. Born in Washington DC, Jen was an adventurous child, climbing play structures and light posts for her first 6 years before moving to Philadelphia in 1980 with her parents and younger sister, Lauren.

Jen grew up as part of the Westview Street gang, a close group of lively neighborhood children who met at the bottom of the beech tree each morning. In high school, Jen captained both the tennis and lacrosse teams graduating from Abington Friends School in 1992. She was on the crew team at the University of Vermont, but when the snow arrived she spent every weekend on the ski slopes, honing her love of dangerous trails at Tuckerman's Ravine.

Jen spent a semester abroad in Aix in Provence, learning French and travelling throughout Europe. After graduating with a B.A. in Sociology from U.V.M., she made the decision to live in Vail for a year. Twenty years later, Jenny had definitely found her niche.

Jen's adventurous spirit took her around the world. Besides her semester in France, she spent time in Israel working in a factory packing helmets, biking through Croatia, teaching English to children in a small town in Kenya, working as an au pare to a family in Verbier, Switzerland and traveling to China, Thailand, Morocco, New Zealand, having adventures that no parent wants to hear about until after their child makes it back safely. She once called from Morocco to ask permission to go to Morocco. She came home with beautiful photographs of her trip.

After moving to Vail, Jen became a ski instructor. She was certified to teach Alpine, Nordic, and Snowboarding. Jen completed a Masters in Teaching from University of Denver, and began working in the Eagle County School Districts, teaching a variety of grades and subjects in several schools. Her creativity flourished through her teaching on and off the mountain.

Jen wrote openly about her struggle with lymphoma through her prose and poetry on her Caring Bridge page. Like everything she did, Jen fought with determination to win this unforgiving battle.

Jen loved her life in Vail. She loved skinning to the top of the mountain and skiing down. She loved the challenge of climbing an ice wall and biking in Moab. But what she loved the most were her special friends and family.

We will miss her beautiful smile, her kind heart and thank her community for making her feel loved.

About the Editors

Jen Pinkus always loved to write. When she was diagnosed with Follicular Lymphoma in April 2015, Jen started an on-line blog/journal choosing the CaringBridge website as her vehicle. CaringBridge is a website that allows family and friends to get updates and offer encouragement to the person in need.

Jen filled her journal with photos, poems and prose about her daily experience dealing with cancer. She was able to put into words her hopes and fears and found peace in the writing. Friends and family wrote heartfelt comments that gave her the courage to fight the disease.

Several people encouraged Jen to publish her blog thinking it would be helpful for other patients and health care workers. Jen lost her battle with lymphoma before she had a chance to think about publishing. Her mother and aunt picked up where Jen left off.

Cheryl Shoag Pinkus holds a Masters of Art in Teaching. She is Jen's mother. Now retired, she taught in the lower school at Germantown Friends School in Philadelphia, PA for 28 years.

Helaine Shoag Greenberg, Jen's aunt, holds a Doctorate of Social Work. Her dissertation title was *Self Esteem in Children Who Survive Cancer*.

CPSIA information can be obtained
at www.ICGtesting.com
Printed in the USA
BVHW061954131118
532948BV00003B/3/P